American Doll Quilts

16 LITTLE PROJECTS THAT HONOR A TRADITION

KATHLEEN TRACY

Martingale®
& COMPANY

American Doll Quilts:
16 Little Projects That Honor a Tradition
© 2004 by Kathleen Tracy

That Patchwork Place® is an imprint
of Martingale & Company®.

Martingale & Company

20205 144th Avenue NE

Woodinville, WA 98072-8478 USA

www.martingale-pub.com

Printed in China

09 08 07 06 05 04   8 7 6 5 4 3 2 1

CREDITS

President: Nancy J. Martin

CEO: Daniel J. Martin

Publisher: Jane Hamada

Editorial Director: Mary V. Green

Managing Editor: Tina Cook

Technical Editor: Laurie Bevan

Copy Editor: Melissa Bryan

Design Director: Stan Green

Illustrators: Robin Strobel and Laurel Strand

Cover and Text Designer: Regina Girard

Photographer: Brent Kane

Library of Congress Cataloging-in-Publication Data
Tracy, Kathleen.
   American doll quilts : 16 little projects that honor a tradition / Kathleen Tracy.
      p. cm.
   Includes bibliographical references.
   ISBN 1-56477-589-5
 1. Patchwork—Patterns. 2. Quilting—Patterns.
 3. Doll quilts. 4. Miniature quilts. I. Title.
   TT835 .T725 2004
   746.46'041—dc22

                                        2004014847

MISSION STATEMENT

*Dedicated to providing quality products
and service to inspire creativity.*

DEDICATION

To Paul, for his never-ending encouragement; to my children, Evan and Caitlin, for helping me remember my own childhood; and to my mother, for always nurturing the child within me.

ACKNOWLEDGMENTS

Special thanks to the wonderful editorial and design staff at Martingale & Company for turning my vision into a reality.

Thanks to Gail Wilson for the use of her amazing dolls in some of the photos.

Thanks to Kathy Parker for allowing us to photograph the quilts on location at her home.

Thanks to my sisters, for "spoiling" me with dolls when I was a child.

I am also grateful to the legions of women from the past who encouraged the art of quilting in their children, keeping this craft tradition alive.

Contents

Preface

I should have been born the daughter of a quilter, but my mother had five girls to raise, and that took up most of her creative energy, I imagine. It wasn't until her later years, when her health wasn't the best and I, the youngest, was out of college, that she found pleasure in crafts like needlepoint, crocheting, and rug hooking.

She did know how to sew, however, because I remember spending time as a young child playing at her feet while they worked the treadle machine. I should have known it was in my future to be a quilter, but I came late to the craft. Fabric has always fascinated me. I can still vividly remember the colors and patterns in the material from my favorite childhood dresses, cotton dresses I wanted to wear over and over again because I loved the colors in the prints and the softness of the fabric. The garments don't exist anymore, except for a few buttons my mother salvaged before she turned the dresses into dust cloths. Yet even these small button souvenirs evoke poignant memories of my past.

Dolls were one of my early passions and, like many women, I find that they, too, rekindle powerful memories of my childhood. It wasn't until I had a daughter, however, that I allowed myself the indulgence of playing with dolls again.

Antique doll quilts are rare today, and their scarcity makes them highly collectible. The quilts that enchant us the most are the ones made by children, and we love these quilts for their ability to invoke powerful memories of childhood with all its simple charm. Doll quilts had lives of their own. They were played with until they frayed, and children's dreams were wrapped up in them as young girls and boys acted out future roles. We can't help but wonder about the lives of the women and children who made and played with these treasured pieces. What stories could each quilt tell?

It's a sad fact that women today often don't have much time for creative pursuits. Women of the past had even less time than we do now, but they were wise enough to know the restorative power of handicrafts and the great stress relief that creative endeavors can provide. With meditation and yoga classes so popular today, contemporary women could use a reminder that quilting itself (especially hand quilting small pieces) takes us into an almost meditative state, releasing tension and unleashing countless creative impulses.

Quilting gives the creator a tremendous sense of satisfaction. The next time you're feeling stressed and the idea of making a large quilt is too much to even think about, start a small quilt and watch the stress disappear. Perhaps share the craft with a child you love. The urge to create is very strong in children, and we need to encourage that desire. Allowing children to be creative—or, better yet, helping them to be creative—inspires creativity within ourselves as well.

I should have been born the daughter of a quilter, but I will be satisfied being the mother of one someday. While all of us who call ourselves quilters hope that our quilts will be cherished and remembered as a legacy for future generations after we're gone, perhaps the real legacy lies in giving our children the gift of knowing *how* to quilt.

Introduction

Lately it seems that quilters everywhere, myself included, have become intrigued by reproduction fabrics and miniatures. What better way to address that interest than by re-creating doll quilt patterns that reflect our love of the past and our wonder about the women who made those quilts? I wrote *American Doll Quilts* to show busy women that they *do* have time to quilt, and that quilting isn't difficult if they start small. Doll quilts can provide a great introduction to quilting while laying a foundation for children to enjoy the craft as they grow older. All the patterns in this book are designed so that a beginning adult or a child (with an adult's help) can easily piece together the quilts by hand or machine.

The quilts are not complex, scaled-down versions of large quilts, but small samplings of quilt blocks used during particular time periods—simple blocks that have been adapted in the same way that makers of doll quilts throughout our history might have done. When you begin to quilt, don't worry too much about whether your blocks are perfect or your seams line up exactly. Have fun and quilt with enthusiasm! After you've made a few quilts, the techniques become easier and progress is inevitable. Look at what you can do!

"A Short History of Doll Quilts," beginning on page 8, looks at the beginnings of quilting in America and the ways the craft has changed over the centuries. "Quilting the Past," starting on page 10, shows you how to choose the best fabrics for your doll quilts to recapture that wonderful old-fashioned look we love in antique quilts. Thereafter, the book is divided into significant periods of American history and the quilts that best represent those times, along with a description of the fabrics common to the age and patterns to make your own doll quilts representative of that era. Re-create your own antiques! "Quilting Basics," on pages 74–77, gives a short lesson on quilting to get you started if you are a beginner.

Quilters from the past would have been delighted to have the abundance of fabrics and patterns we have to choose from today. I hope that this book will encourage women to experience the joy of quilting by making some or all of these quilts, while understanding the traditions of the past and acknowledging women's quilting as a remarkable expression of their lives.

A Short History of Doll Quilts

Quilting has played a significant role in American history and in American women's lives from the time the first English settlers brought their needlework skills with them to the New World. What role did doll quilts play in that history, and why are they so cherished today? According to Deborah Harding, in *America's Glorious Quilts,* "Antique doll quilts are among the most collectible textiles today. One may pay more for a doll quilt in good condition than for a full-size quilt of the same pattern and date."

What exactly is it about doll quilts that has stirred interest not only among folk-art enthusiasts but among women everywhere? Not many of these small quilts have survived, which could account for some of the demand among serious collectors. But I suspect there is more to the fascination among quilters and non-quilters alike.

Until the beginning of the twentieth century, sewing was a skill every woman needed to know and was often taught to girls before reading and writing. There was a time when almost every woman quilted and was expected to teach her daughters to do the same. Doll quilts were used as practice for most young girls' sewing skills, since needlework and sewing were considered an important part of a girl's education. It is difficult for us to imagine a time when most girls were already experienced in the art of sewing by the age of 15, and many began the craft at the age of 4 or 5.

A female's self-esteem was often tied up in her needlework skills, and accomplished young women concentrated their energies on needlework instead of scholarly endeavors in the nation's early schools. In the nineteenth century, it was understood in some quarters that a young woman, from the time she started quilting, was expected to make 13 quilts before she was married as proof of her readiness for matrimony and managing a household.

While today we might make a small quilt for a decorative purpose or to hang on a wall, such was not the case years ago, when bed quilts were necessary to keep the family warm. Crafts such as quilting were an important part of a child's life in early America. Life was often hard, and with most tasks done by hand, children were expected to help out as much as they were able. Learning to sew and practicing on doll quilts meant a child could help with the family's daily sewing chores. Quilts were made out of necessity, often stitched in all-too-few quiet moments after a long, hard day of work.

Some doll quilts were made by mothers for their children, but we assume most were made by the children themselves, to make sewing exercises more fun and help children gain a certain sewing expertise that would be useful as an adult. Crib quilts made by adults most often were intended as heirlooms, and the ones that survive have little wear and tear. Doll quilts, however, suffered much rigorous use, and the scrappy look they embody is proof that expensive fabrics and fancier stitches were saved for other quilts.

Many of the doll quilts that quilters seem to treasure today are not accomplished specimens made with expert stitches, but rather the ones made by children, with their simple, often crude stitches and uncomplicated patterns.

These projects were often made with scraps because, by necessity, mothers saved their costlier fabrics for fancier quilts and clothing. While larger quilts are appreciated for their complexity and intricacy, their rich use of textiles and color, and their excellent needlework, doll quilts have a different appeal—they call out to our emotions. We see a child's frustration of trying to master little stitches and striving for accuracy. We treasure the laborious stitches because we know how much hard work went into them. We're touched by the simplicity and earnestness of the completed project.

What a sense of pride these young quilters must have experienced! What new quilter hasn't felt the same childlike pride upon completing her first quilt, no matter how small? I also sympathize with the frustrations children surely felt on their paths to becoming better quilters. Doll quilts embody the child within us all and speak to us of our own childhoods and emerging creative expressions.

In a sense, America's quilting heritage is in its doll quilts because they reflect the beginner in every one of us. Doll quilts are at the heart of every great quilt ever made. Every quilter had to begin somewhere, and we can only guess how many learned to quilt at their mother's knee.

There is probably no woman today who would disagree that the modern age places many demands on our time. One way to balance it all out is to bring beauty and simplicity into our surroundings. By filling our homes with remembrances of childhood, we are also filling our hearts. So let's decorate with the things we love, and in doing so try to recall some of the moments of childhood. If there is a lesson we can learn from the doll quilts of the past, it must be to accept the beauty of simplicity and to bring all of the wonders of childhood into our hearts.

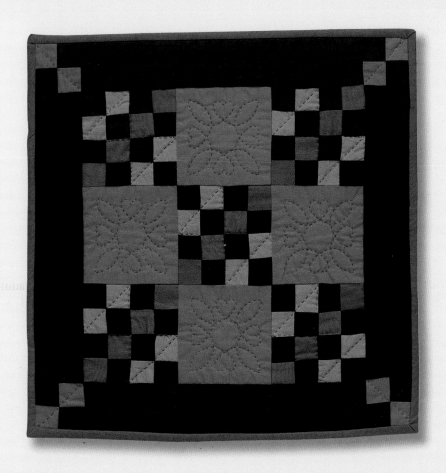

Quilting the Past

It's a common, but unfortunate, misconception that all antique quilts were made in shades of dull brown. You can witness this idea in the many reproduction quilts today that use sepia tones to represent the past. While it's true that different periods of quilting history popularized deep tans and chocolate browns, quilts of long ago also contained fabrics with rich and varied colors. The creators of these quilts did not originally choose brown as the predominant hue. Instead, the browns so often seen were actually purples, reds, and even greens that softly faded as the many natural dyes, often made from plants and tree bark, lost their color and vibrancy over time.

The small quilts in this book attempt to capture some of that vibrancy and the types of fabric that may have originally been present in antique quilts. As modern-day quilters, we have the wonderful advantage of being able to choose from the enormous array of reproduction fabrics available.

Many antique doll quilts, although not all, use small-scale prints. Such prints are important in making small quilts because there are fewer blocks to work with than in a larger project. Like many quilters today, I like to combine these little prints with medium- or larger-scale designs and a selection of geometrics, stripes, plaids, or checks for contrast and liveliness in the overall look of the quilt. Using too many large-scale prints gives the quilt a sense of "busyness," so it's a good idea to save those fabrics for quilt borders.

QUICK TIP

Many fabric stores have remnant bins or scrap baskets, which are excellent for finding small pieces of fabric in varying shades and prints for making small quilts. I am sometimes drawn to a certain small piece of fabric that might be just the touch to offset other fabrics in a quilt. By using small amounts of a large variety of fabrics, we can achieve the scrappy look that is so common in quilts made years ago.

By choice, I don't prewash my fabrics before piecing. I find that the slight shrinkage that occurs upon washing the finished quilt gives the piece an aged appearance. Instead of soaking the entire quilt in a tea bath to give it an antique feel, I individually tea stain small pieces of the brighter fabrics that need to be muted before they're pieced into blocks. (See the tip about tea dyeing on page 11.) Because many of the reproduction fabrics available now have that muted look, I don't tea dye too often. However, if certain fabrics in your stash look too bright when placed next to others, tea dyeing them individually is an easy way to avoid making other pieces look more aged than they already are. This way, the tans and off-whites don't become too dark as well. Washing a small quilt gently by hand will also give it an old-fashioned look without distorting the colors too much.

QUICK TIP

For tea dyeing, place three tea bags in a large bowl (any black tea will do). Bring one quart of water to a boil and pour it over the tea bags. Let the tea steep for 15 minutes then remove the bags. Add any fabric pieces you wish to dye and let them soak for 10 to 20 minutes, depending on how dark you wish to make them. Rinse the fabrics in cool water and squeeze out any excess. Air-dry or press with a hot iron to speed up the drying time.

You will want to use 100%-cotton fabric when making your small quilt, with the exception of "Victorian Crazy Quilt" on page 50, which uses silk and satin fabrics. Since there is less room for error when making small quilts, I prefer to use fabrics that have a certain amount of stiffness because they are less likely to fray and are easier to cut and piece accurately.

In many of the quilts in this book, I avoid uniformity among the blocks by using varied prints in shades of the same color. This enhances the antique feel of the projects, since quilts of long ago were frequently made from whatever scraps were available at the time. If one type of fabric ran out, a similar one took its place. In addition, scrap quilts often contain unique color combinations—fabrics you would not normally think of placing next to each other might actually work well together. Who would think of using black in a predominantly pastel quilt, or placing purple next to red? Yet quilters before us used color schemes like these to produce lively results and a certain flow of color in their quilts.

One important thing to remember about making quilts with a vintage look is to generally avoid the use of white, bright-colored, or contemporary fabrics. Instead of white, many antique quilts contain colors such as tan or off-white. Unless you are reproducing quilts from the forties, which often used white as a background for very bright or pastel feedsack fabrics, use tan or off-white to balance small prints or for backgrounds in blocks. Too much brightness in a certain fabric creates a stark contrast with adjacent colors. Instead, use darker colors to add contrast, such as black or gray geometrics or darker shades of blue, brown, green, or red in differing intensities. Many of my quilts use varying shades of blue as a neutral, calming ingredient. Shirtings, consisting of an allover design on a white or light background (used to make men's shirts), were also very popular in antique quilts and are another important element in making quilts with an aged quality.

Another characteristic to consider when choosing fabric is value, which is the relative lightness or darkness of a fabric. Value is often what makes different colors look so pleasing when placed next to each other. Strive for a pattern of light and dark values throughout the quilt to create a vintage-looking softness.

In summary, remember these tips for small-quilt success:

- Rely on small-scale prints with a splash of geometrics, stripes, plaids, or checks, and an occasional large-scale print.

- Choose muted colors, not brights, for an antique look. If there is a fabric you really like and it appears too bright, tea dye the piece you plan to use to slightly dull and soften the color.

- Use light tan or off-white for backgrounds.

- Create contrast by using darker hues of the same colors used in the quilt instead of large prints or bright fabrics.

Making small quilts gives us an opportunity to experiment with different color schemes or fabrics without expending a tremendous amount of time or money. Be creative and try using your own color choices and fabrics to give a unique look to some of the quilts in this book.

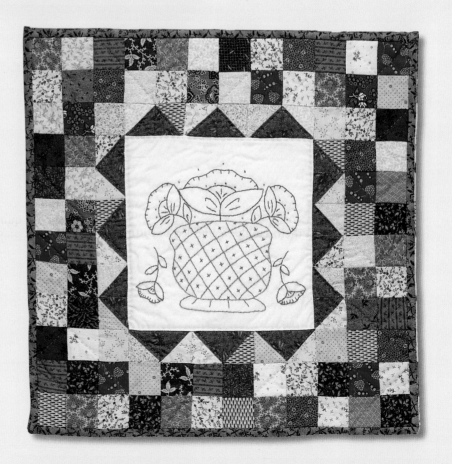

Early America
(1776–1820)

The first thing we realize when looking at quilts from this early period of American history is that quilting was not common. Few quilts remain, and the ones that have survived are in museums or private collections and are rarely seen. The exquisite quilts from this time show a life of refinement for those who could afford it.

Life was difficult for most of the early settlers, however. Most items were made by hand and, as fabric was still imported from England and France, the cost was often prohibitive. With spinning and weaving necessary to make cloth, women had little incentive to spend their time sewing quilts when ready-made bed coverings were available from England. The common image of women settlers pursuing quilting in their spare time is probably a false one. Women had little time for leisure pursuits and plain sewing was the rule. Children were often recruited at the early ages of five or six to help with these daily chores, because sewing and mending for the family were never-ending tasks.

In early America, reading and writing were considered far less important to a woman than learning how to run a household. The needlework skills women had learned in England, however, proved to be a valuable tradition to pass on to their daughters and led to future quilting.

Quilts made during this period appear in three styles—whole cloth, *broderie perse,* and central medallion. Whole cloth quilts were usually made of solid-colored fabric, often white, and quilted with intricate needlework, displaying the skills many of the women brought with them from overseas.

Broderie perse, or Persian embroidery, consisted of creating an appliqué motif from pieces of chintz fabric containing flowers, birds, vines, or butterflies, and then cutting out the shapes and sewing them to a plain fabric. This central design was then surrounded by a floral border. *Broderie perse* was probably the beginning of the appliqué style that became so common in American quilts later in the nineteenth century.

The central-medallion quilt was the prevailing type of quilt made during this period. These quilts consisted of embroidery or floral appliqué in the middle surrounded by rows of geometric patchwork shapes, mostly squares and right triangles. This form was probably the beginning of the simple block tradition that defines American quiltmaking today.

Fabric continued to be imported from England until the first American textile mills opened in 1790. As fabric became available and more affordable, quilting became more widespread and women's creativity flourished. Soon after, in the early nineteenth century, the block style was developed and, along with fabric availability, forever influenced quiltmaking in America.

Broderie Perse Quilt

Finished Quilt Size: 18¾" x 18¾"

Inspired by some of the medallion-style coverlets of the late eighteenth and early nineteenth centuries, this little quilt uses the appliqué technique of broderie perse, or Persian embroidery, to display the chintz and toile prints popular in early America. Because fabric was imported from France or England, it was expensive and often hard to come by. Early American women cut motifs from small portions of these expensive fabrics and appliquéd them to more modest fabrics to decorate and dress up their quilts or coverlets.

MATERIALS

Yardages are based on 42"-wide, 100%-cotton fabrics.

¾ yard of red-and-cream print for appliqué background and quilt backing

⅜ yard of blue-and-red floral for appliqué and outer border

¼ yard of red-and-white toile print for center block

¼ yard of blue-green fabric for center block

¼ yard of dark red print for inner border and binding

¼ yard of blue striped floral for middle border

22" x 22" piece of batting

¼ yard of lightweight fusible web

CUTTING

From the red-and-white toile print, cut:
1 square, 5" x 5"

From the blue-green fabric, cut:
2 squares, 4" x 4"; cut once diagonally to yield four triangles

From the dark red print, cut:
1 strip, 1" x 42"; crosscut into 2 pieces, 1" x 6¾", and 2 pieces, 1" x 7¾"

2 binding strips, 1⅜" x 42"

From the red-and-cream print, cut:
1 square, 22" x 22"

2 squares, 6" x 6"; cut once diagonally to yield four triangles

From the blue striped floral, cut:
2 strips, 1½" x 42"; crosscut into 2 pieces, 1½" x 10¾", and 2 pieces, 1½" x 12¾"

From the blue-and-red floral, cut:
2 strips, 3½" x 42"; crosscut into 2 pieces, 3½" x 12¾", and 2 pieces, 3½" x 18¾"

ASSEMBLY

1. Sew blue-green triangles to the top and bottom of the toile square, pressing the seam allowances toward the triangles. Sew matching triangles to the sides of the square and then press again. Trim this center block to 6¾" x 6¾". Be sure to leave a ¼" seam allowance past each point of the toile square.

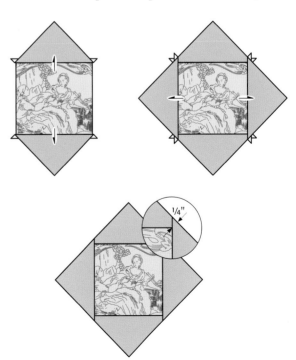

2. Sew the 6¾" red strips to two sides of the center block, pressing the seam allowances toward the red strips. Sew the 7¾" red strips to the other two sides and then press again.

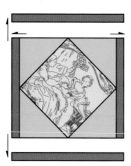

3. Sew the red-and-cream triangles to two opposite sides of the block, pressing the seam allowances toward the triangles. Sew matching triangles to the remaining sides and then press again. Trim this block to 10¾" x 10¾", being sure to leave a ¼" seam allowance past each point of the inner red border.

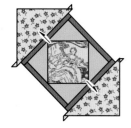 

4. Sew the 10¾" blue striped floral strips to the sides of the block, pressing the seam allowances toward the floral strips. Sew the 12¾" blue striped floral strips to the top and bottom of the block and then press again.

5. Add the 12¾" blue-and-red floral strips to the top and bottom of the quilt center, pressing the seam allowances toward the outer borders. Sew the 18¾" blue-and-red floral strips to the sides and then press again.

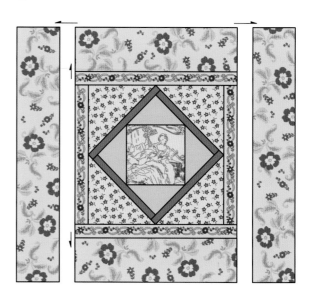

6. For the *broderie perse* appliqué, cut four floral motifs from the leftover blue-and-red floral. Choose designs that are approximately the same size and that are small enough to fit nicely in the red-and-cream corners of the quilt top. Referring to "Fusible Appliqué" on pages 75–76, fuse the selected flowers onto the corners. If desired, stitch the appliqués to the fabric using matching thread; or, simply leave them as they are, and after the batting and backing have been layered, quilt an outline stitch 1/16" from the flowers to make the motifs stand out.

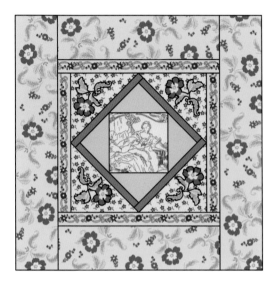

FINISHING

1. Layer the quilt top, batting, and backing, and baste the layers together as shown in "Putting the Quilt Together" on page 76.

2. Echo quilt around the toile square and outline quilt 1/16" from the *broderie perse* flowers. Quilt in the ditch on both sides of the blue striped floral borders, and quilt with straight lines in a diagonal pattern in the outer border.

3. Attach the binding to the quilt referring to "Single-Fold Binding" on page 77.

TIPS FOR *BRODERIE PERSE*

Motifs suitable for *broderie perse* can be found at almost any fabric store. When you shop for fabrics, look for large floral prints that contain flowers, birds, vines, or butterflies, as in the chintz patterns of the past, and be sure to choose colors that appeal to you. I use one of the many types of fusible-web products on the market today to simply fuse the appliqué pieces onto my background fabric. Some quilters may wish to add an embroidery stitch around the appliqué shape, but I find that since the quilt will probably be hung on a wall and not get much practical use, the fusible web alone works fine.

Medallion Quilt

Finished Quilt Size: 18½" x 18½"

Before the traditional block quilt evolved, medallion quilts were common. They often featured a central motif that was either embroidered or appliquéd and surrounded by borders consisting of squares or triangles in a frame style. Early American women brought their extensive needlework skills with them from abroad, and the embroidery was a way to show off their talents.

MATERIALS

Yardages are based on 42"-wide, 100%-cotton fabrics.

1 fat quarter of muslin or off-white fabric for background

¼ yard of teal blue print for triangle frame

¼ yard *total* of assorted dark fabric scraps for borders

¼ yard *total* of assorted light fabric scraps for borders

⅝ yard of backing fabric

¼ yard of brown fabric for binding

22" x 22" piece of batting

Embroidery thread in red, blue, green, and gold

Embroidery hoop (optional)

CUTTING

From the muslin or off-white fabric, cut:
1 square, 9½" x 9½"

From the dark fabric scraps, cut:
40 squares, 2" x 2"

From the light fabric scraps, cut:
44 squares, 2" x 2"

12 squares, 2⅜" x 2⅜"

From the teal blue print, cut:
12 squares, 2⅜" x 2⅜"

From the brown fabric, cut:
2 strips, 1⅜" x 42"

ASSEMBLY

1. Using a sharp pencil or water-soluble pen, lightly trace the embroidery design on page 21 onto the 9½" muslin or off-white square. Embroider the design using an outline stitch and French knots with a single strand of embroidery thread in the colors shown in the diagram on page 21. Use a small embroidery hoop if desired.

French Knot

Outline Stitch

2. Sew 40 of the light 2" squares and all of the dark 2" squares into 20 four-patch units as shown, randomly placing the lights and darks. Press the seams of adjoining pairs in opposite directions, and then press the final seam of each unit in either direction.

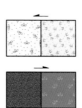

Make 20.

3. Layer each 2⅜" light square on top of a 2⅜" teal square, right sides together. Draw a diagonal line across each light square. Stitch ¼" from the line on

both sides, and cut on the drawn line. Press the seams toward the teal fabric.

Make 24.

4. Sew the triangle squares together into four strips as shown. Press the seams in one direction.

Make 4.

5. Sew two of the triangle strips to the sides of the embroidered square, orienting the teal triangles as shown below. Press the seams toward the center square.

6. Sew the four remaining 2" light squares to each end of the two remaining triangle strips, and press the seams toward the squares. Sew these strips to the top and bottom of the embroidered square, orienting the teal triangles as shown. Press the seams toward the center square.

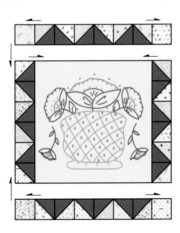

7. Sew eight of the four-patch units into two strips as shown. Sew these strips to the sides of the quilt center, and press the seams toward the four-patch strips.

8. Sew the 12 remaining four-patch units into two additional strips, and sew these to the top and bottom of the quilt center. Press the seams toward the four-patch strips.

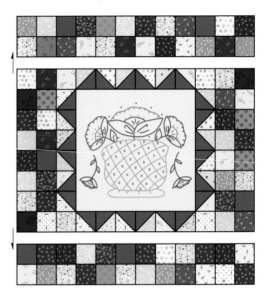

FINISHING

1. Layer the quilt top, batting, and backing, and baste the layers together as shown in "Putting the Quilt Together" on page 76.

2. Quilt in the ditch along the edge of the embroidered square and on the outside edge of the teal triangles. Quilt an X through the center of each four-patch block.

3. Attach the binding to the quilt referring to "Single-Fold Binding" on page 77.

Embroidery Design

○ French knot

— Outline stitch

Liberty Pillow

Finished Pillow Size: 6½" x 6½"

Early American girls were expected to practice their needlework skills almost daily. Making little projects was fun, and patriotic political sentiments of the day often found their way into the pieces. The skills learned as children helped the girls become expert needlewomen when they grew up.

MATERIALS

Yardages are based on 42"-wide, 100%-cotton fabrics.

Assorted scraps of red, blue, and tan prints for borders

Scrap of muslin for embroidery background

Scrap of fabric for pillow back

Embroidery thread in blue and red

Polyester fiberfill

Embroidery hoop (optional)

CUTTING

From the muslin, cut:
1 square, 4" x 4"

From a red print, cut:
1 piece, 2" x 4"

From two different blue prints, cut:
1 piece, 2" x 4"

1 piece, 2" x 7"

From a tan print, cut:
1 piece, 2" x 7"

From the backing fabric, cut:
1 square, 7" x 7"

ASSEMBLY

1. Sew the red and blue 2" x 4" pieces to the sides of the muslin square, pressing the seam allowances toward the border pieces. Sew the tan and blue 2" x 7" pieces to the top and bottom and then press again.

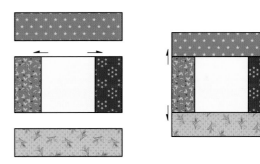

2. Place the muslin square over the lettering pattern below left and trace lightly with a pencil or water-soluble pen. Using one strand of embroidery floss, backstitch the letters in blue and the stars in red. An embroidery hoop is recommended.

Backstitch

3. Place the backing fabric on top of the block, right sides together. Using a ¼" seam, sew around the edges, leaving a 2" opening for turning. Turn the pillow right side out and stuff with fiberfill. Slipstitch the opening closed.

Embroidery Design

Going West
(1830–1850)

The expansion west occurred during a significant period of growth for America. It was a time of growth for the tradition of quilting as well, and vast numbers of quilts were made during this period. Beginning with the development of textile mills in America in the late eighteenth and early nineteenth centuries, and the subsequent wide availability of fabric, interest in quilting surged. Later, in 1840, the invention of the treadle sewing machine revolutionized the craft. Even though these early machines were foot-powered, they saved enormous amounts of time previously spent hand piecing.

Because the population of the United States was increasing at such a fast rate, the push westward was inevitable. Cities on the East Coast became crowded, and good farming land was either scarce or expensive—or both. Encouraged by cheap land and the promise of opportunity and fortune, early settlers from the East accepted the challenge and headed west. The pioneer women who joined the trek brought along quilts they had made in preparation for the journey as well as quilts received as gifts from beloved friends and family. Thus began the popularity of the friendship quilt, sometimes called the signature quilt, signed with love as families, friends, and neighbors faced separation. These quilts were often prized for the memories and touch of home they offered during times of loneliness in new surroundings. Other quilts were used to brighten up otherwise drab, often primitive, households and as practical covers for drafty windows and doors.

Life on the frontier was often lonely and desolate. It was especially so for the women, who were expected to shoulder certain burdens alone without the support or companionship of extended family while the men worked long hours to make new lives. Pioneer women were on much more equal footing with men than their urban counterparts, and the stereotypical image of the stalwart frontierswoman was not a myth. Many of them developed great strength of character through the often back-breaking work necessary to withstand the hardships involved in wilderness life. They knew that only by sharing the daily workload with the men could their

family's success be assured. This meant hours of cleaning, cooking, sewing, tending the vegetable garden, and raising the children. Quilting was a necessity. Families were often large so that there would be more helping hands, but that also meant more beds that required blankets for warmth.

Since one's nearest neighbors might live miles away, social occasions were limited, and quilting bees became a popular way to alleviate some of the loneliness and make life bearable for the pioneer women. While they were a wonderful chance to visit with neighbors, quilting bees were functional as well. Quilts from this era were often pieced by one woman but quilted by many, and frequently new friendships were formed as women who might have had nothing else in common drew together in a communal endeavor. Quilting offered a respite from feelings of despair and isolation while providing one of the only outlets for creative fulfillment.

It was during this time that the block method of quilting emerged. Precipitated by the invention of the sewing machine, and further aided by the growing availability of fabric at general stores in frontier towns, the block method soon came to typify the American style of quiltmaking. Many new block patterns were developed on the trail west, with names like Broken Dishes, Bear's Paw, Schoolhouse, and, much later, Log Cabin, often reflecting the settlers' daily experiences.

Salvaging scraps and trading blocks became a pioneer tradition. Borders were commonly used to piece together blocks that were shared or pieced by others. Around this time, quilters added more color contrast to quilts than before, perhaps to make the blocks stand out, again defining and fixing the style of the traditional American quilt. Many of the quilts we see from this era used bright shades of red and blue because these were the colors that retained their vividness while others faded.

Quilting had become established as an American tradition by the middle of the nineteenth century, and today we owe a debt to the women who followed their creative hearts and, with their strength and energies, left us an enduring history of their lives in the fabric they pieced.

Prairie Quilt

Finished Quilt Size: 15" x 16½" • Finished Block Size: 4" x 4"

Life wasn't easy for the pioneers as they settled the West. Fabric was scarce and quilters used up every scrap they could find to piece together their quilts. Young girls learned how to piece their first quilts using simple designs like this one.

MATERIALS

Yardages are based on 42"-wide, 100%-cotton fabrics.

¼ yard of dark blue checked fabric for borders

¼ yard *total* of assorted pink, blue, and brown print scraps for blocks

¼ yard *total* of assorted shirtings or light print scraps for blocks

½ yard of backing fabric

¼ yard of pink print for binding

18" x 20" piece of batting

CUTTING

From the assorted pink, blue, and brown prints, cut:
18 squares, 2½" x 2½"

From the assorted shirtings or light prints, cut:
18 squares, 2½" x 2½"

From the blue checked fabric, cut:
1 strip, 2½" x 42"; crosscut into 2 pieces, 2½" x 12½"

1 strip, 1¾" x 42"; crosscut into 2 pieces, 1¾" x 16½"

From the pink print, cut:
2 strips, 1⅜" x 42"

ASSEMBLY

1. From the assorted colored and light print 2½" squares, sew two dark and two light squares together as shown to make a four-patch unit, pressing the seams of each pair toward the dark squares. Make nine units, pressing the final seam in either direction.

Make 9.

2. Sew the four-patch blocks together into three rows of three blocks each. Refer to the illustration that follows and to the quilt photograph for placement of the dark and light squares, if desired. Press the seams in the opposite direction from row to row. Sew the rows together and press the seams in one direction.

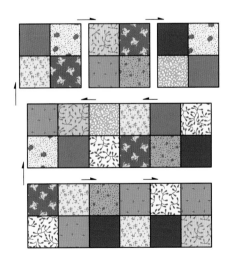

3. Sew the 2½" blue checked strips to the top and bottom of the quilt center, pressing the seam allowances toward the borders.

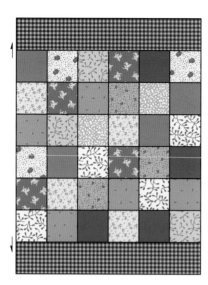

4. Sew the 1¾" blue checked strips to the sides of the quilt center and then press again.

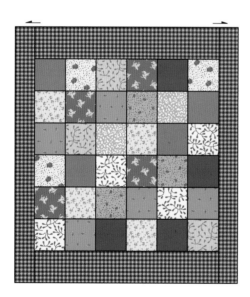

FINISHING

1. Layer the quilt top, batting, and backing, and baste the layers together as shown in "Putting the Quilt Together" on page 76.

2. Quilt through the center of each square, vertically and horizontally, and through the middle of each border.

3. Attach the binding to the quilt referring to "Single-Fold Binding" on page 77.

Strippy Triangles

Finished Quilt Size: 13½" x 18" • Finished Block Size: 1¾" x 1¾"

Piecing triangles together from scraps and assembling them into strips provided an easy way for little girls to learn sewing skills. Scrap quilting became a new American tradition, reflecting the resourceful spirit of the pioneers as they faced the harsh realities of life on the frontier.

MATERIALS

Yardages are based on 42"-wide, 100%-cotton fabrics.

⅜ yard *total* of assorted shirtings or light print scraps for blocks

⅛ yard of pink print for blocks

⅛ yard of medium blue print for blocks

⅛ yard of dark blue print for blocks

⅛ yard of gold print for blocks

⅛ yard of blue-green print for blocks

⅛ yard of red print for blocks

⅛ yard of gold or tan print for borders

½ yard of backing fabric

¼ yard of small blue print for binding

17" x 21" piece of batting

CUTTING

From the assorted shirtings or light prints, cut:
30 squares, 2¾" x 2¾"

From the pink print, cut:
5 squares, 2¾" x 2¾"

From the medium blue print, cut:
5 squares, 2¾" x 2¾"

From the dark blue print, cut:
5 squares, 2¾" x 2¾"

From the gold print, cut:
5 squares, 2¾" x 2¾"

From the blue-green print, cut:
5 squares, 2¾" x 2¾"

From the red print, cut:
5 squares, 2¾" x 2¾"

From the gold print, cut:
1 strip, 1¾" x 42"; crosscut into 2 pieces, 1¾" x 18"

From the small blue print, cut:
2 strips, 1⅜" x 42"

ASSEMBLY

1. Layer each of the assorted light 2¾" squares on top of a print 2¾" square, right sides together. Draw a diagonal line across each light square. Stitch ¼" from the line on both sides and cut on the drawn line. Press the seams toward the dark fabric. Trim each block to 2¼" x 2¼".

Make 10
each color.

2. Sew 10 triangle squares of the same color into a vertical row as shown. Repeat to make six rows, each a different color. Arrange the rows side by side, referring to the illustration for color placement. Press the seams in opposite directions from row to row.

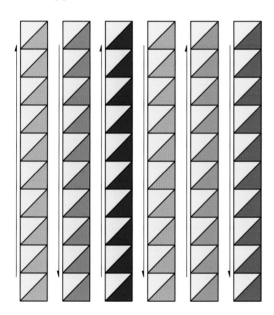

3. Sew the rows together as shown to make the quilt center. Press the seams in one direction.

4. Sew the 18" pieces of gold or tan print to the sides of the quilt center and press the seams toward the borders.

FINISHING

1. Layer the quilt top, batting, and backing, and baste the layers together as shown in "Putting the Quilt Together" on page 76.

2. Quilt diagonal lines through the center of the blocks as shown. You may also wish to quilt in the ditch along the inside edge of each border.

3. Attach the binding to the quilt referring to "Single-Fold Binding" on page 77.

Red and Blue Shoo Fly

Finished Quilt Size: 13½" x 17" • Finished Block Size: 4½" x 4½"

Pioneer life was lonely and often desolate. Women turned to quilting for comfort and community. Quilting bees became a popular way for entire families to gather and socialize. Quilts made from scraps in bright colors like turkey reds and indigo blues were a way of giving a pioneer cabin a cheerful, homey look.

MATERIALS

Yardages are based on 42"-wide, 100%-cotton fabrics.

⅛ yard of red-and-white checked fabric for borders

⅛ yard of blue print for borders

Scraps of 3 different red prints for blocks

Scraps of 3 different blue prints for blocks

Scraps of 6 different shirtings or light prints for blocks

½ yard of backing fabric

¼ yard of red print for binding

17" x 20" piece of batting

CUTTING

From 4 of the shirtings or light prints, cut:
2 squares, 2⅜" x 2⅜" (8 squares total)

4 squares, 2" x 2" (16 squares total)

From 1 of the remaining shirtings or light prints, cut:
4 squares, 2⅜" x 2⅜"

6 squares, 2" x 2"

From the remaining shirting or light print, cut:
2 squares, 2" x 2"

From *each* red print, cut:
2 squares, 2⅜" x 2⅜" (6 squares total)

1 square, 2" x 2" (3 squares total)

From *each* blue print, cut:
2 squares, 2⅜" x 2⅜" (6 squares total)

1 square, 2" x 2" (3 squares total)

From the red-and-white checked fabric, cut:
1 strip, 2½" x 42"; crosscut into 2 pieces, 2½" x 14"

From the blue print for borders, cut:
1 strip, 2" x 42"; crosscut into 2 pieces, 2" x 13½"

From the red print for binding, cut:
2 strips, 1⅜" x 42"

ASSEMBLY

1. Layer each 2⅜" light square on top of a 2⅜" red or blue print square, right sides together. Draw a diagonal line across each light square. Stitch ¼" from the line on both sides, and cut on the drawn line. Press the seams toward the dark fabric.

Make 24.

2. Sew four matching triangle squares, a matching 2" square, and four matching 2" light squares together as shown to make three red blocks and three blue blocks. Press the seams within each row toward the light squares, and press the row seams toward the center. The top left block and the bottom right block use the same light print, except for two

squares in the bottom right block, which are a different light print. You can see this clearly in the photograph on page 32.

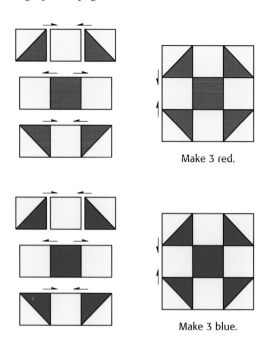

Make 3 red.

Make 3 blue.

3. Sew the blocks together into three rows of two blocks each as shown. Press the seams in the opposite direction from row to row. Sew the rows together, and press the seams in one direction.

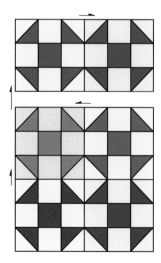

4. Sew the 14" checked pieces to the sides of the quilt, pressing the seam allowances toward the borders. Sew the 13½" blue pieces to the top and bottom of the quilt and press again.

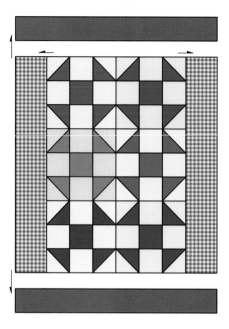

FINISHING

1. Layer the quilt top, batting, and backing, and baste the layers together as shown in "Putting the Quilt Together" on page 76.

2. Quilt an X through the center of each block and quilt in the ditch around each block. Quilt through the middle of each border.

3. Attach the binding to the quilt referring to "Single-Fold Binding" on page 77.

Friendship Pillow

Finished Pillow Size: 5½" x 5½"

> *Friendship quilts were gifts from friends and relatives to pioneer families headed west. These pieces were special because they carried the signatures and sentiments of those left behind, easing the loneliness of the new experience on the frontier.*

MATERIALS

Yardages are based on 42"-wide, 100%-cotton fabrics.

Assorted scraps of pink, blue, tan, and brown prints for pillow top

Scrap of coordinating fabric for pillow back

Scrap of muslin for quilted lining

6" x 6" piece of batting

Polyester fiberfill

Freezer paper (optional)

CUTTING

From the blue scraps, cut:
1 square, 2⅞" x 2⅞"

From the tan scraps, cut:
3 squares, 2⅞" x 2⅞"

1 square, 2½" x 2½"

From the pink scraps, cut:
2 squares, 2⅞" x 2⅞"

From the brown scraps, cut:
2 squares, 2⅞" x 2⅞"

From the muslin, cut:
1 square, 6" x 6"

From the fabric for pillow back, cut:
1 square, 6½" x 6½"

ASSEMBLY

1. Layer the blue square with a 2⅞" tan square, right sides together, with the lighter square on top. Draw a diagonal line across the light square. Stitch ¼" from the line on both sides and cut on the drawn line. Press the seam toward the darker fabric.

2. Repeat step 1 using the following pairs of fabrics: a pink square with a 2⅞" tan square, a pink square with a brown square, and a brown square with a 2⅞" tan square.

3. Arrange the triangle squares and the 2½" tan square as shown to form a Friendship Star block. Sew the squares into rows, pressing the seams as shown.

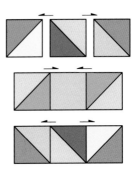

4. Sew the rows together, and press the seams toward the center.

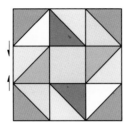

5. If you wish to add signatures, iron a piece of freezer paper to the wrong side of the block. This stabilizes the fabric and makes writing easier. Have friends or family members sign the block using a permanent-ink marker, and then remove the freezer paper.

6. Layer the block with the batting and the muslin square. Quilt ¼" around the star and inside the center square.

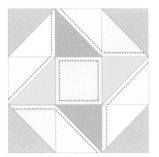

7. Place the backing fabric on top of the quilted pillow front, right sides together. Using a ¼" seam, sew around the edges, leaving a 2" opening for turning. Turn right side out and stuff with fiberfill. Slip-stitch the opening closed.

Quilted Comfort
(1861–1865)

The Civil War may well have been the worst war in our nation's history, certainly causing more deaths than any other, and the pain it inflicted is evident in the quilts that came out of it. The 1860s were trying times for America, and the many roles that women played are mirrored in their quilts. Quiltmakers were prolific because the need for quilts was immense. Unfortunately, most of the women's efforts are lost to history—not many of their quilts survived, and we can assume that many were discarded from heavy use or buried along with the men who died.

Before the war even began, as early as the 1830s, many women dedicated their voices and quilts to the abolitionist movement. Anti-slavery fairs, much like our craft bazaars today, moved these women to action and made use of their considerable needlework skills through the thousands of quilts made and sold for the cause. Women did not have the vote, but they used their quilts to make political statements about those issues that concerned them most, often inscribing patches with written sentiments. One quilt pattern in particular—the Underground Railroad—reflects some women's views on

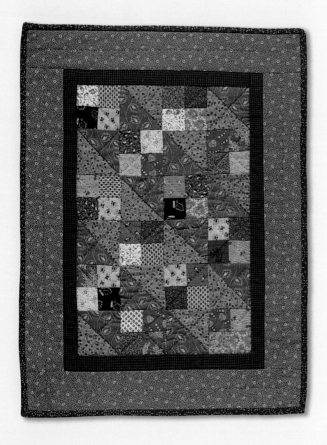

slavery, and even today this pattern survives as a testament to the courage of many during this troubled time.

An abundance of stories have been written about the Underground Railroad and the quilts that are said to have been used to help slaves escape to freedom in the North. The Underground Railroad was not an actual railroad, but an organization consisting of free blacks and whites who sympathized with and aided slaves attempting to flee. Safe houses were supposedly those that displayed a Log Cabin quilt with a black center square, and when these quilts were hung in a window or on a clothesline, slaves could be assured of a hiding place on their journey. Certain quilt blocks conveyed information about when to leave and what paths to take. The actual Underground Railroad pattern, with its light and dark contrasting squares placed in an ascending formation, is said to point to specific directions for escape.

Historians disagree on whether the signal codes involving quilts are fact or fiction. The Log Cabin quilt pattern, for instance, did not become popular until well after the Civil War and probably originated as a tribute to the memory of President Lincoln and his boyhood home. Other than oral records and stories passed down from families, there does not seem to be much evidence that these quilts played such a role. Yet secrecy and signals must certainly have been a part of this venture, and the missions may not have succeeded without them. The question of whether the quilts held secret signs is a fascinating one, however, and I have included a pattern for the Underground Railroad design in this book. In any case, whether the messages hidden in the pattern are fact or fiction, it stands as a wonderful tribute to the role that many women and their quilts played in an important stage of American history.

When the first shots were fired in the war and thousands of men enlisted to join the fight, women were left at home to shoulder the burden of running the farms and businesses. They soon felt compelled to do something else to help. Soldier's Aid Societies, providing food, clothing, and bedding for the troops, urged women to sew for the soldiers. It is estimated that 100,000 of the more than 200,000 quilts made for the military were distributed through the Sanitary Commission, the forerunner of the American Red Cross, to soldiers' beds and hospitals. Quilts were also made to be raffled off to raise funds for the war effort. Some of the quilts donated were exquisite examples of fine needlework and raised substantial amounts of money. Others were made from scraps and sewed with a sense of urgency because they were so desperately needed.

The loss of loved ones is conveyed in the colors of the quilts made during this time—dark, somber hues mixed with grays and blacks. The Civil War is one period when brown shades, called madder browns, were dominant. Bright colors such as turkey reds, cheddars, purples, and double pinks were mixed with darker colors, called mourning fabrics, and then plaids, stripes, or paisley prints were added to produce quilts with a distinctive look. Because many of the dyes used were fugitive (that is, likely to change over time), the once-bright colors have now faded to drab brown. Indigo blue was also a common choice, probably because of its colorfast properties.

Quiltmaking after the Civil War grew out of necessity as a devastated nation struggled with a drained economy. Fabric was scarce and expensive—most of it had gone to support the war. Scrap quilts reached a new height of popularity as economic times worsened.

Sadly, few quilts from this period have survived. The ones that have been salvaged tell their stories through their unique colors and patterns. We may have forgotten the names of the quilters, but history won't let us forget the significant role that women and their quilts played in the Civil War.

Underground Railroad

Finished Quilt Size: 19" x 25" • Finished Block Size: 6" x 6"

During the years before the Civil War, many women gave their voices to the anti-slavery movement. Quilt patterns such as the Underground Railroad may represent the network of safe houses for slaves on their journey to freedom. Many myths surround the quilts made during this time. Some say that secret messages were pieced in the cloth, while others disclaim the notion that quilts played any part in the movement. Nevertheless, this pattern is an important tribute to the courage of those who changed history.

MATERIALS

Yardages are based on 42"-wide, 100%-cotton fabrics.

¼ yard of deep blue Civil War reproduction print for blocks

¼ yard of gold Civil War reproduction print for blocks

¼ yard of dark red check for inner border

¼ yard of medium blue fabric for outer border

¼ yard *total* assorted scraps of light and dark Civil War reproduction prints for blocks

⅞ yard of backing fabric

¼ yard of brown fabric for binding

22" x 28" piece of batting

CUTTING

From the assorted light and dark Civil War prints, cut:
48 squares, 2" x 2"

From the deep blue Civil War print, cut:
6 squares, 3⅞" x 3⅞"

From the gold Civil War print, cut:
6 squares, 3⅞" x 3⅞"

From the red check, cut:
2 strips, 1¼" x 42"; crosscut into 2 pieces, 1¼" x 12½", and 2 pieces, 1¼" x 20"

From the medium blue fabric, cut:
2 strips, 3" x 42"; crosscut into 2 pieces, 3" x 20", and 2 pieces, 3" x 19"

From the brown fabric, cut:
3 strips, 1⅜" x 42"

ASSEMBLY

1. Randomly sew the light and dark 2" squares together into 12 four-patch units as shown, pressing the seam allowance of each pair in opposite directions. When joining pairs to make a four-patch unit, press the seam in either direction.

Make 12.

2. Layer each 3⅞" blue square with a 3⅞" gold square, right sides together, with the lighter square on top. Draw a diagonal line across each light square. Stitch ¼" from the line on both sides and cut on the drawn line. Press the seams toward the blue fabric.

Make 12.

3. Sew two triangle squares and two four-patch units together as shown, pressing the seam in each pair toward the four-patch unit. When joining the pairs, press the seam in either direction.

 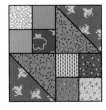

Make 6.

4. Arrange the blocks in three rows of two blocks each as shown to make the quilt center. Sew the blocks together into rows, and press the seams in opposite directions from row to row. Sew the rows together, and press the seams in one direction.

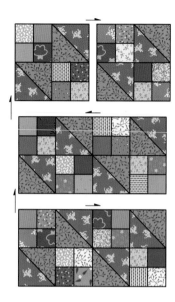

5. Sew the two 12½" checked pieces to the top and bottom of the quilt center, pressing the seam allowances toward the checked pieces. Sew the two 20" checked pieces to the sides and then press again.

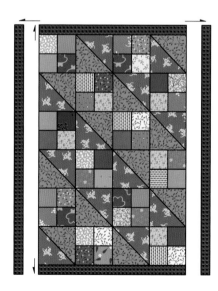

6. Sew the two 20" medium blue pieces to the sides of the quilt top as shown above right, pressing the seam allowances toward the outer border. Sew the two 19" medium blue pieces to the top and bottom of the quilt top and then press again.

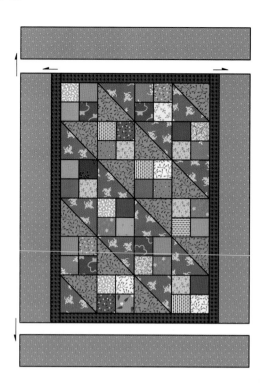

FINISHING

1. Layer the quilt top, batting, and backing, and baste the layers together as shown in "Putting the Quilt Together" on page 76.

2. Quilt an X through the center of each block and quilt in the ditch around the inside and outside edges of the inner border. Quilt through the middle of the outer border.

3. Attach the binding to the quilt referring to "Single-Fold Binding" on page 77.

Civil War Nine Patch

Finished Quilt Size: 18½" x 25½" • Finished Block Size: 6" x 6"

The Civil War gave birth to some of history's most beautiful quilts. Quilts were made from scraps and sewed with a sense of urgency because they were so desperately needed. Not many have survived, either due to extreme wear or because they were buried along with the men who gave their lives.

MATERIALS

Yardages are based on 42"-wide, 100%-cotton fabrics.

¼ yard of red print for borders

¼ yard of blue print for borders

Scraps of 18 different dark or medium Civil War reproduction fabrics for blocks

Scraps of 9 different light Civil War reproduction fabrics for blocks

½ yard of backing fabric

¼ yard of gray fabric for binding

22" x 29" piece of batting

CUTTING

From *each* of the light Civil War fabrics, cut:
4 squares, 2" x 2" (36 squares total)

From 9 of the dark or medium Civil War fabrics, cut:
4 rectangles, 2" x 3½" (36 rectangles total)

From the remaining dark or medium Civil War fabrics, cut:
1 square, 3½" x 3½" (9 squares total)

From the red print, cut:
1 strip, 2½" x 42"; crosscut into 2 pieces, 2½" x 18½"

From the blue print, cut:
1 strip, 2" x 42"; crosscut into 2 pieces, 2" x 18½"

From the gray fabric, cut:
3 strips, 1⅜" x 42"

ASSEMBLY

1. Arrange four matching 2" light squares, four matching 2" x 3½" dark or medium rectangles, and one contrasting 3½" dark or medium square as shown. Sew the pieces into rows, pressing the seams of the top and bottom rows toward the corner squares and the seams of the middle row toward the center square. Sew the rows together and press the seams toward the center.

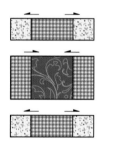 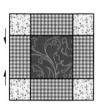

Make 9.

2. Arrange the blocks in three rows of three blocks each. Sew the blocks into rows, pressing the seams in the opposite direction from row to row. Sew the rows together and press the seams in one direction.

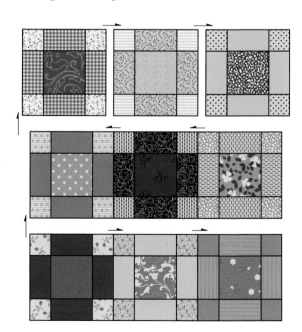

3. Sew the two 18½" red pieces to the top and bottom of the quilt center and press toward the red border. Sew the two 18½" blue pieces to the red pieces and press toward the blue border.

FINISHING

1. Layer the quilt top, batting, and backing, and baste the layers together as shown in "Putting the Quilt Together" on page 76.

2. Quilt an X through the center of each block and quilt through the middle of the red borders. Quilt in the ditch on the inside edge of the blue borders.

3. Attach the binding to the quilt referring to "Single-Fold Binding" on page 77.

Civil War Needle Case

Finished Needle Case Size: 3" x 3"

A needle case was a common household item during the nineteenth century. A larger version of this simple one, called a "housewife," contained needles, thread, buttons, and scissors, and was sent along with a soldier to keep in his haversack for repairing socks and uniforms as necessary.

MATERIALS

Scrap of Civil War reproduction print for case cover

Scrap of shirting or light print for case lining

Scrap of coordinating print for pockets

Scrap of coordinating felt for needle holder

Scrap of neutral-colored felt for batting

CUTTING

From the print for pockets, cut:
2 rectangles, 2½" x 3½"

From the shirting or light print, cut:
1 rectangle, 3½" x 7"

From the Civil War print, cut:
1 rectangle, 3½" x 7"

From the neutral-colored felt, cut:
1 rectangle, 3½" x 7"

From the felt for needle holder, cut:
1 rectangle, 2½" x 5"

ASSEMBLY

1. Fold under one long side of both coordinating-print rectangles by ¼" and press. Fold under ¼" again, press, and stitch to hem the pockets.

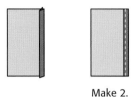

Make 2.

2. Place each pocket piece on either side of the 3½" x 7" light print rectangle, right sides up, and pin in place.

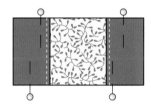

3. Layer the 3½" x 7" Civil War print rectangle and the 3½" x 7" light print rectangle right sides together. Place the rectangle of neutral-colored felt on the bottom. Using a ¼" seam, sew the layers together, leaving a 1" opening for turning.

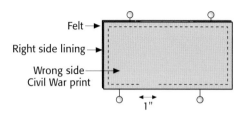

Felt →
Right side lining →
Wrong side →
Civil War print
1"

4. Turn the needle case right side out and press flat. Fold the seam allowances at the opening to the inside and sew completely around the case, ⅛" inside the edge.

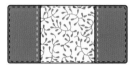

5. Center the coordinating 2½" x 5" piece of felt on the inside of the open needle case and stitch a line down the middle. Close the case and press.

The Gilded Age (1876–1900)

The end of the nineteenth century brought immense changes for Americans, and for women in particular. Although much of America faced severe hardship after the Civil War, few could imagine what was ahead for the country as the nineteenth century closed. Dramatic social and economic changes took place as industrial growth and new technology thrust the United States forward. Urban growth, transportation, and improved standards of living transformed the nation. The frontier was settled, America became a melting pot, and the country rushed headlong into a new era. Great fortunes were made during this time and the Gilded Age is representative of that wealth.

Quiltmaking in America dropped dramatically, at least in urban areas where ready-made blankets and other manufactured items were widely available in department stores and through mail-order catalogs. With increased wealth came more time for recreation. Leisure pastimes became status symbols, and women whose husbands could afford it had help with household duties, freeing up time formerly spent on domestic chores such as sewing. Even in non-urban areas, the invention of the sewing machine a few decades earlier saved a tremendous amount of time. Sewing that previously required so much effort could now be accomplished much more quickly and easily, allowing Victorian quilters the opportunity to develop other needlework skills, such as fancy embroidery. These skills often became an indicator of a woman's social position since only the more affluent could afford the time to spend on them. At the turn of the century, women looked for more stylish ways to decorate their homes and were strongly influenced by the ladies' magazines of the day. Gilded Age style was showy to the point of gaudy, and many front parlors featured an excessive array of decorative items, symbols of status to many. The most popular quilt style during this time was the Crazy Quilt, a wild display that seemed to parallel the changing role of women in society. No longer obliged to produce the family's bed coverings, women of the time steered their sewing skills into creative arenas, making quilts solely for ornamentation. Quilting emerged as a hobby, not a necessity, and women's individuality in the arts was unleashed.

The Philadelphia Centennial Exposition of 1876 had perhaps the strongest influence on quilts made during this time and was responsible for an upsurge in interest in the craft. Celebrating America's first hundred years, the Exposition displayed exhibits from all around the world. Eager for new ideas from different cultures, visitors crowded exhibits such as the one from Japan. It may have been the oriental ceramics with their glazed, cracked finishes, or the kimonos and large panels randomly pieced with silks and finished with elegant needlework seen in these exhibits that started the Crazy Quilt trend. Whatever the influence, American women responded by creating Crazy Quilts with a passion. Pieced haphazardly to catch the eye, Crazy Quilts featured fancy dress fabrics like silks, velvets, and brocades placed in sometimes severe patterns and finished with exquisite needlework. Dark colors prevailed in the quilts, probably as a result of Queen Victoria's mourning after the death of her husband, Albert. England's Queen Victoria, influential in America as well as overseas, loved embroidery, and she inspired the intricate designs of some of these pieces.

Crazy Quilting is perhaps one of the most distinctive styles of American quilting. These richly embroidered quilts, with their kaleidoscope qualities, reflected the greater freedom and creativity women were experiencing at this time. Progress brought with it greater educational and employment opportunities for women and chances to pursue interests outside the home. Aware of the impact their united efforts had on the abolitionist movement of the past, American women came together to pursue better lives for themselves. Still denied the vote, women's suffrage groups began to proliferate and, after the turn of the century, women looked for fulfillment in areas other than domestic ones. American life was changing, and as old ideas faded, along with old-fashioned quilt patterns, the role of women in society began to change as well.

Victorian Crazy Quilt

Finished Quilt Size: 12½" x 12½" • Finished Block Size: 4½" x 4½"

The decorative style of the Gilded Age was showy to the point of gaudiness. The Crazy Quilt is one of the most unusual and eye-catching styles of American quilting. These richly embroidered quilts, with their kaleidoscope qualities, gave women the license to be creative in their fabric choices and show off their needlework skills.

MATERIALS

¼ yard of muslin for block foundations

¼ yard *total* of silk, satin, and brocade scraps for blocks

⅛ yard *each* of 2 different black prints for borders

½ yard of backing fabric

¼ yard of black fabric for binding

16" x 16" piece of batting

Gold thread for embellishment stitches

CUTTING

From the muslin, cut:
4 squares, 5" x 5"

From *different* silk, satin, and brocade scraps, cut:
4 center pieces from the pattern on page 54

From *one* of the black prints, cut:
1 strip, 2" x 42"; crosscut into 2 pieces, 2" x 9½"

From the remaining black print, cut:
1 strip, 2" x 42"; crosscut into 2 pieces, 2" x 12½"

From the black fabric for binding, cut:
2 strips, 1⅜" x 42"

ASSEMBLY

1. Using a pencil, trace the pattern on page 54 onto the wrong side of each of the muslin squares and number the patches.

2. Place a center piece right side up over patch 1 on the right side of one muslin square. Looking from the wrong side of the muslin square, you will be able to see the raw edges of piece 1 to be sure the piece evenly covers the sewing lines with ¼" seam allowances.

Right side of muslin   Wrong side of muslin

3. Choose a different silk, satin, or brocade fabric and cut a piece that is large enough to cover patch 2, including ¼" seam allowances. Place it right side down over patch 1, aligning the raw edges as shown, and pin to hold in place. From the wrong side of the muslin square, sew the pieces together along the line between patch 1 and patch 2, starting one stitch into patch 5 and ending one stitch into patch 3. Fold the muslin foundation back out of the way and trim any excess fabric beyond the ¼" seam allowance of these two pieces. On the front, fold piece 2 over to the right side and press lightly with a warm, not hot, iron.

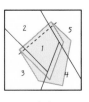
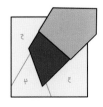

Stitch.   Press.

4. Choose a different fabric and cut a piece that is large enough to cover patch 3, including ¼" seam allowances. Place piece 3 right side down over patches 1 and 2, aligning the raw edge of the piece ¼" past the seam line (look from the wrong side of the muslin square to align this piece correctly). Pin to hold in place. From the wrong side of the muslin square, sew the pieces together along the line connecting with patch 3, starting one stitch into patch 4 and stitching to the edge of the muslin square. Fold the muslin foundation back out of the way and trim any excess fabric beyond this ¼" seam allowance. On the front, fold piece 3 over to the right side and press lightly.

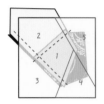 

5. Choose a different fabric and cut a piece that is large enough to cover patch 4, including ¼" seam allowances. Place piece 4 right side down over patches 1 and 3, aligning the raw edge of the piece ¼" past the seam line (look from the wrong side of the muslin square to align this piece correctly). Pin to hold in place. From the wrong side of the muslin square, sew the pieces together along the line connecting with patch 4, starting one stitch into patch 5 and stitching to the edge of the muslin square. Fold the muslin foundation back out of the way and trim any excess fabric beyond this ¼" seam allowance. On the front, fold piece 4 over to the right side and press lightly.

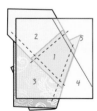 

6. Choose a different fabric and cut a piece that is large enough to cover patch 5, including ¼" seam allowances. Place piece 5 right side down over patches 1, 2, and 4, aligning the raw edge of the piece ¼" past the seam line (look from the wrong side of the muslin square to align this piece correctly). Pin to hold in place. From the wrong side of the muslin square, sew the pieces together along the line connecting with patch 5, stitching from one edge of the muslin square to the other edge. Fold the muslin foundation back out of the way and trim any excess fabric beyond this ¼" seam allowance. On the front, fold piece 5 over to the right side and press lightly.

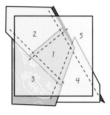 

7. Repeat steps 2 through 6 to make three more blocks using different fabrics in each of the patch positions. Trim all of the blocks to 5" x 5".

8. Sew the blocks together as shown, rotating them so that they are not all in the same position. Press the two rows in opposite directions and press the row seam in either direction.

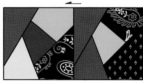

9. Using decorative stitches on your sewing machine or fancy stitches by hand, embroider along all the seams of the patches with gold thread. Sew a decorative stitch along the horizontal and vertical seams connecting the blocks. Add decorative monograms or designs with the same gold thread, or try other colors that match your Crazy Quilt.

QUICK TIP

Women of the Gilded Age sometimes embellished their Crazy Quilts with lace, ribbon, beads, personal mementos, buttons, or charms.

FINISHING

1. Layer the quilt top, batting, and backing, and baste the layers together as shown in "Putting the Quilt Together" on page 76.

2. Quilt in the ditch around the perimeter of the blocks.

3. Attach the binding to the quilt referring to "Single-Fold Binding" on page 77.

10. Sew the 9½" black print pieces to the sides of the quilt top, pressing the seam allowances toward the borders. Sew the 12½" black print pieces to the top and bottom of the quilt top and then press again.

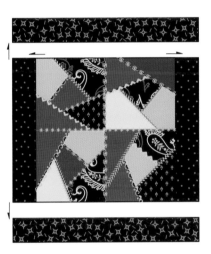

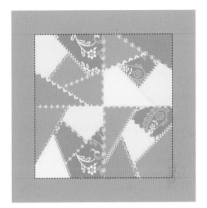

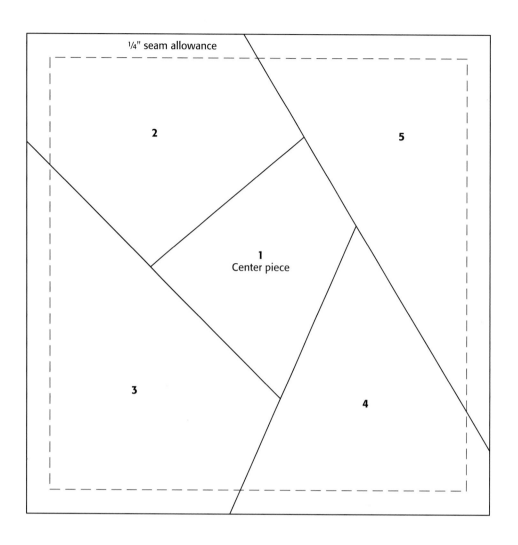

¼" seam allowance

2

5

1
Center piece

3

4

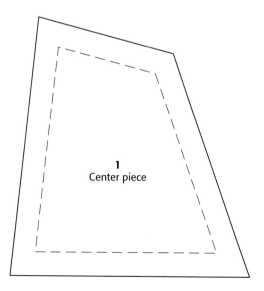

1
Center piece

Indigo Blue and White Quilt

Finished Quilt Size: 14½" x 18½" • Finished Block Size: 4" x 4"

Quilters in the Gilded Age still loved indigo fabric, and shades of blue pieced with white were featured in many of the quilts produced at the end of the nineteenth century. Just about every quilter had a blue-and-white quilt with fancy quilting she saved for a special occasion or made as an heirloom to celebrate a wedding or birth. Indigo is a colorfast dye, and its popularity continues to this day.

MATERIALS

Yardages are based on 42"-wide, 100%-cotton fabrics.

¼ yard of dark indigo print for inner border

¼ yard of white-and-blue print for outer border

¼ yard *total* of assorted indigo prints for blocks

¼ yard *total* of assorted white-and-blue prints or shirtings for blocks

½ yard of backing fabric

¼ yard of dark blue fabric for binding

18" x 22" piece of batting

6 buttons

⅛"-wide dark blue ribbon (optional)

CUTTING

From the assorted indigo prints, cut:
12 squares, 3¼" x 3¼"

From the assorted white-and-blue prints or shirtings, cut:
12 squares, 3¼" x 3¼"

From the dark indigo print, cut:
2 strips, 1" x 42"; crosscut into 2 pieces, 1" x 9½", and 2 pieces, 1" x 12½"

From the white-and-blue print, cut:
2 strips, 3" x 42"; crosscut into 2 pieces, 3" x 13½", and 2 pieces, 3" x 14½"

From the dark blue fabric, cut:
2 strips, 1⅜" x 42"

ASSEMBLY

1. Layer each indigo print square with a white-and-blue square, right sides together, with the light square on top. Draw a diagonal line across each light square. Stitch ¼" from the line on both sides and cut on the drawn line. Press the seams toward the darker fabric. Cut these squares on the diagonal as shown to make two triangle units from each square. Sew the triangle units together as shown and press the seams in either direction to make 24 hourglass units.

Make 24.

2. Sew the hourglass units into six blocks as shown, alternating the shades of indigo. Press the seams of each pair in opposite directions and press the joining seam in either direction.

Make 6.

3. Arrange the blocks in three rows of two blocks each as shown. Sew the blocks into rows, and press the seams in opposite directions from row to row. Sew the rows together and press the seams in one direction.

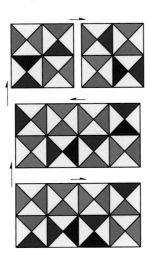

4. Sew the two 12½" indigo pieces to the sides of the quilt center, pressing the seams toward the border. Sew the two 9½" indigo pieces to the top and bottom of the quilt center and then press again.

5. Sew the two 13½" white-and-blue pieces to the sides of the quilt top, pressing the seams toward the outer border. Sew the two 14½" white-and-blue pieces to the top and bottom of the quilt top and then press again.

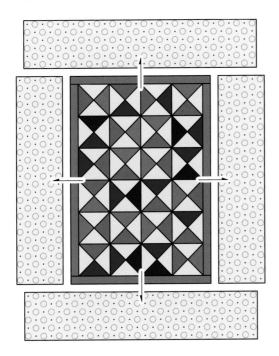

FINISHING

1. Layer the quilt top, batting, and backing, and baste the layers together as shown in "Putting the Quilt Together" on page 76.

2. Quilt in the ditch around the six pinwheel blocks as shown. Quilt in the ditch around the outside edge of the inner border. Quilt the outer border as desired. I used a decorative stitch on my sewing machine to stitch through all three layers with dark blue decorative thread. If you choose, make four bows with the dark blue ribbon and tack them to the corners of the outer border as shown in the quilt photograph. Sew a button in the center of each pinwheel.

3. Attach the binding to the quilt referring to "Single-Fold Binding" on page 77.

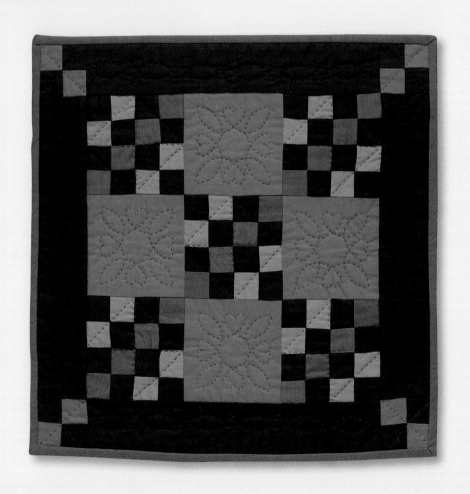

America at War & The Twenties (1914–1929)

After the Gilded Age, quilting experienced yet another decline. The two decades leading up to the 1920s became the age of independence for women—their leisure interests turned elsewhere as they entered the work force and their duties were no longer tied so closely to the home. American women won the right to vote in 1920, and with that achievement came a degree of freedom from previously strict standards of behavior. There were those who looked upon the many freedoms women had gained and saw quilting and needlework as oppressive. During this time America also became a consumer society. Fashion took hold of women in the middle class, and quilting and sewing were looked upon as quaint, old-fashioned pursuits, pastimes that were popular mostly in rural areas of the country.

World War I began in Europe in 1914. When the United States entered the war in 1917, women once again took up their needles for the war effort as they had during the Civil War. Reminded of the impact their efforts had made then, many women turned to quilting in some capacity to support their country. The Red Cross urged women to quilt to raise funds for the war effort; the federal government urged women to quilt for the home in order to conserve manufactured blankets for the military. As in other times of conflict, this period of the Great War encouraged women to express their patriotism through quilting. Women pieced red-white-and-blue banners and star quilts for display in their windows to indicate a family member serving his country. Other women quilted as a way to keep busy while waiting for loved ones to come home.

The 1920s saw a resurgence in quilting that was a direct result of the colonial revival movement, a trend that sparked a renewed interest in American handicrafts and folk art. People became interested in collecting antiques, and quilts were recognized as valuable examples of early American art. The arts and crafts movement during this time showed that handmade crafts were worthy of being called "art." Design schools were established to provide education and training in the arts, and doors were opened for women to enter the business world in new, creative ways.

Women continued to draw upon various sources for their quilting patterns. Many traditional patterns were mass produced and widely distributed in the 1920s. In addition to magazines, newspapers began to print patterns on a regular basis, and some of them published favorite patterns sent in by readers. Quilt kits also became available, either through mail-order catalogs or off store shelves.

While quiltmaking declined in mainstream America during the early part of the twentieth century, it increased in the Amish community. The Amish quilts that are so collectible today were made during this time, and it is rare to find one from the nineteenth century. There are few quilt styles so striking in America's quilt history as the Amish quilt. This very distinctive style seems to have been influenced by the dark, somber colors of the Victorian era. The Amish took many traditional block patterns that had been popular up to this point and combined them with vivid solid colors pieced with black.

Amish quilting has hardly wavered from the traditional patterns relied upon years ago. Unlike their "English," or non-Amish, neighbors, Amish women had no interest in women's rights or other political issues, and their time was spent refining the techniques used in quilting simple patterns. They were more likely to experiment with new color palettes that became available instead of trying new trends. The starkness of some quilt borders often reveals incredible hand quilting. The vibrant colors and simple yet extraordinary designs convey the creativity of Amish women, despite a culture that discourages individual expression.

To many outsiders, the Amish community seems restrictive. Yet their traditions, faith, and simplicity in living reflect a world that values family and community above all. Because quiltmaking is practical and necessary, it is an acceptble creative outlet. In studying Amish plain designs we see evidence of a remarkable group of female quilters who elevated simplicity to a new level of art.

Star Medallion

Finished Quilt Size: 15½" x 15½" • Finished Block Size: 5" x 5"

During World War I, quilters liked to use reds, whites, and blues in patterns that proudly displayed patriotism in unconventional and creative ways.

MATERIALS

Yardages are based on 42"-wide, 100%-cotton fabrics.

¼ yard *total* of 6 different red prints for blocks

¼ yard *total* of 7 different blue prints for blocks

½ yard *total* of 5 different light tan prints for blocks

½ yard of fabric for backing

¼ yard of blue fabric for binding

19" x 19" piece of batting

CUTTING

From *each of 2* of the red prints, cut:
1 square, 3" x 3" (2 squares total)

From *each of 3* of the red prints, cut:
8 squares, 1¾" x 1¾" (24 squares total)

From the *remaining* red print, cut:
4 strips, 2⅛" x 5½"

From *each of 3* of the blue prints, cut:
1 square, 3" x 3" (3 squares total)

From *each of 2* of the blue prints, cut:
8 squares, 1¾" x 1¾" (16 squares total)

From *each of the remaining* blue prints, cut:
2 strips, 2⅛" x 5½" (4 strips total)

From *each of 3* of the light tan prints, cut:
4 squares, 1¾" x 1¾" (12 squares total)

4 rectangles, 1¾" x 3" (12 rectangles total)

From 1 of the *remaining* light tan prints, cut:
8 squares, 1¾" x 1¾"

8 rectangles, 1¾" x 3"

From the *remaining* light tan print, cut:
4 strips, 2⅛" x 5½"

From the blue fabric for binding, cut:
2 strips, 1⅜" x 42"

ASSEMBLY

Three of the Star blocks are made up of one 3" blue square, four matching 1¾" x 3" light tan rectangles, four matching 1¾" squares of the same light tan as the rectangles, and eight matching 1¾" red squares. Two of the Star blocks are made up of one 3" red square, four matching 1¾" x 3" light tan rectangles, four matching 1¾" squares of the same light tan as the rectangles, and eight matching 1¾" blue squares. The top right and lower left Star blocks have the same light tan background.

1. Lay out the sets of fabrics for each block in advance. Draw a diagonal line across each red and blue 1¾" square on the wrong side of the fabric.

2. To make each block, place one 1¾" square on top of one end of a 1¾" x 3" rectangle, right sides together, as shown. Sew on the line and trim to a ¼" seam allowance. Press the triangle toward the corner. Place another square on the other end of the rectangle, right sides together, and stitch on the drawn line. Be sure the diagonal line is oriented in the opposite direction from the first piece. Trim to a ¼" seam allowance and press the triangle toward the corner. Make a total of four of these flying-geese units.

Make 4.

3. Sew a light tan square to each end of two of the flying-geese units as shown and press the seams toward the squares. Sew two flying-geese units to each side of the 3" square and press the seams toward the square. Sew these rows together and

press the seams toward the center row. Repeat steps 2 and 3 to make a total of five star blocks.

Make 5.

4. Sew the red, blue, and light tan 2⅛" x 5½" strips together as shown to make a total of four blocks. Press the seams in one direction toward the red strips. Trim these blocks to 5½" x 5½".

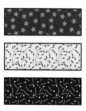 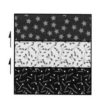

Make 4.

5. Sew the star blocks and the striped blocks together into three rows as shown, placing the blue strips closest to the center star. The blue strips of the same fabric are on opposite sides of the center Star block. Press the seams of each row toward the striped block. Sew the rows together and press the seams toward the middle row.

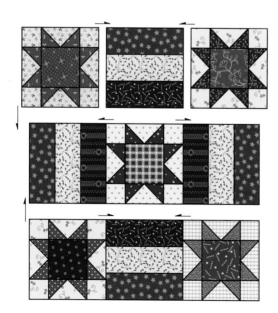

FINISHING

1. Layer the quilt top, batting, and backing, and baste the layers together as shown in "Putting the Quilt Together" on page 76.

2. Quilt an X through the center of each Star block and quilt in the ditch around each star. Quilt through the middle of each blue and light tan stripe.

3. Attach the binding to the quilt referring to "Single-Fold Binding" on page 77.

Amish Nine Patch

Finished Quilt Size: 16½" x 16½" • Finished Block Size: 4" x 4"

The Amish are known for their strict, plain style of living, but their quilts are anything but plain. Their quilts combine traditional patterns with vibrant colors tempered with black. Many Amish women are excellent needle artists, and the dark, plain fabrics display their hand-quilting talents.

MATERIALS

Yardages are based on 42"-wide, 100%-cotton fabrics.

⅜ yard of solid black fabric for blocks and borders

¼ yard of solid pink fabric for blocks

¼ yard of solid purple fabric for blocks and binding

⅛ yard of solid blue-green fabric for blocks

⅝ yard of solid fabric for backing

20" x 20" piece of batting

CUTTING

From the black fabric, cut:
2 strips, 2½" x 42"; crosscut into 4 pieces, 2½" x 12½"

2 strips, 1½" x 42"; crosscut into 48 squares, 1½" x 1½"

From the blue-green fabric, cut:
1 strip, 1½" x 42"; crosscut into 20 squares, 1½" x 1½"

From the purple fabric, cut:
1 strip, 1½" x 42"; crosscut into 20 squares, 1½" x 1½"

2 binding strips, 1⅜" x 42"

From the pink fabric, cut:
1 strip, 4½" x 42"; crosscut into 4 squares, 4½" x 4½", and 8 squares, 1½" x 1½"

ASSEMBLY

1. Sew the blue-green 1½" squares and 20 of the black 1½" squares together to make 10 four-patch units as shown, pressing the seams of each pair toward the black square and the final joining seam in either direction.

Make 10.

2. Sew the purple 1½" squares and 20 of the black 1½" squares together to make 10 four-patch units as shown, pressing the seams of each pair toward the black square and the final joining seam in either direction.

Make 10.

3. Sew two blue-green four-patch units together with two purple-and-black four-patch units as shown to make a total of five blocks, pressing the seams of each pair in opposite directions and the final joining seam in either direction.

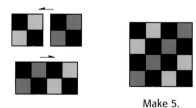

Make 5.

4. Arrange the pieced blocks together with the pink 4½" squares as shown. Be sure the purple squares form a diagonal line from the bottom left to the top right in each block. Sew the blocks into rows and press the seams of each row toward the pink squares. Sew the rows together and press the seams toward the middle row.

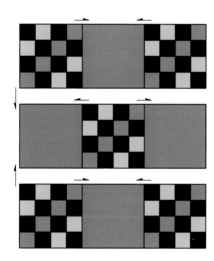

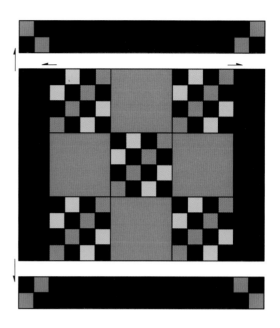

5. Sew the remaining 1½" black squares and the pink 1½" squares together to make four-patch units as in step 1. Make 4. Sew these four-patch units to the ends of two of the 12½" black pieces as shown, being careful that the pink squares will radiate diagonally from the corners of the quilt center when these borders are sewn to the quilt top. Press the seams toward the black pieces.

Make 2.

6. Sew the two plain 12½" black pieces to the sides of the quilt, pressing toward the borders. Sew the border strips from step 5 to the top and bottom of the quilt and then press again.

FINISHING

1. Layer the quilt top, batting, and backing, and baste the layers together as shown in "Putting the Quilt Together" on page 76.

2. Quilt a medallion-style motif in the center of each large pink square. Quilt an on-point square in the middle of each pieced block and quilt an X in each pink-and-black four-patch unit. Quilt a cable-type design in the black border strips.

3. Attach the binding to the quilt referring to "Single-Fold Binding" on page 77.

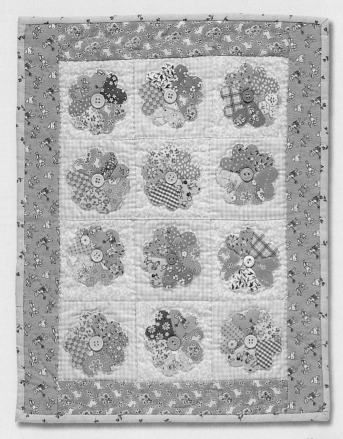

The Great Depression & America at War Again (1930–1945)

If there is one thing that surprises us about quilts made during the 1930s, it is the startling contrast between the bright colors and light backgrounds and the trying times Americans were facing. The events of 1929 that led to the Great Depression caused incredible hardships throughout the country, and women once again turned to quilting out of necessity. The nation was faced with shortages all around and quilting fabric was no exception. As families were encouraged to make do with what they had, quilt tops were patched, and remnants of worn clothing or household linens found their way into the quilts of this era. Yet, despite the poverty that gripped the nation, this was an unusually rich period for quilting. Women looked to the past for strength, and found courage in the ways the pioneers had dealt with adversity. Scrap quilting methods were revived and became a symbol of the thrifty values held by many Depression-era women. The "feedsack" print is the most common fabric that appeared. Used to hold items such as flour, sugar, rice, and animal feed, these brightly patterned cotton bags were collected and chosen with sewing and quilting projects in mind. It is not difficult to identify quilts from this time period—their pastel prints and floral appliqué give testimony to the resilient spirit of the American women who survived trying times. Although it's hard to tell, some of the most beautiful quilts that came out of this period were made out of necessity and as antidotes to despair.

When World War II arrived, quilting underwent another downturn. Textile production fell off as factories and businesses concentrated on manufacturing supplies for the war. Women moved into jobs in offices and factories to replace the men who went to war. The most dedicated quilters still came together in groups to make quilts for the relief effort, but by and large quilting ceased in all but the most rural areas. The years after the war saw women concentrating on building new, modern lives for their families, and store-bought bedding was preferred.

Although quilting has had its ups and downs, it never disappeared from the American landscape completely. In 1976, the year of America's Bicentennial, revived interest in American history and handicrafts from the past brought a whole new generation of quilters to the art form. Today, we hang quilts on walls instead of making them out of necessity.

In looking at the quilts of the past and trying to understand the times in which they were made, we can't help but feel a sense of connection with and pride for the women who made them. Quilting in America has survived more than 200 years, and the current trend promises to keep the tradition alive for a long, long time.

Feedsack Flower Garden

Finished Quilt Size: 14" x 17½" • Finished Block Size: 3½" x 3½"

Americans faced trying times in the 1930s, yet the quilts created during this period were remarkably optimistic, featuring pastels, bright colors, and light backgrounds. Families were encouraged to get by with what they had, and it was not unusual for scraps of worn clothing and household linens to make their way into quilt tops. Quilting experienced a revival as women turned to handmade items to endure the Great Depression.

MATERIALS

Yardages are based on 42"-wide, 100%-cotton fabrics.

¼ yard of pink-and-white checked fabric for block backgrounds

¼ yard of light pink print for block backgrounds

¼ yard *total* of assorted pastel 1930s reproduction scraps for blocks

⅛ yard of green 1930s reproduction print for borders

⅛ yard of medium pink 1930s reproduction print for borders

⅝ yard of backing fabric

¼ yard of yellow print for binding

17" x 21" piece of batting

¼ yard of lightweight fusible web

12 assorted pastel buttons

CUTTING

From the pink-and-white checked fabric, cut:
6 squares, 4" x 4"

From the light pink print, cut:
6 squares, 4" x 4"

From the medium pink 1930s reproduction print, cut:
1 strip, 2" x 42"; crosscut into 2 pieces, 2" x 11"

From the green 1930s reproduction print, cut:
1 strip, 2" x 42"; crosscut into 2 pieces, 2" x 17½"

From the yellow print, cut:
2 strips, 1⅜" x 42"

ASSEMBLY

1. Referring to "Fusible Appliqué" on page 75, trace 60 hearts from the pattern on page 70 onto the fusible web. Cut out the pieces and remove the paper backing. Fuse the shapes to the wrong sides of the assorted pastel reproduction fabrics following the manufacturer's directions for the fusible web. Cut out the hearts.

2. Mark a dot at the center of each 4" square. Use five hearts, each from a different fabric, to make the flowers. Place the hearts on a square, positioning the points at the dot. The edges of the hearts will overlap. Fuse the hearts in place leaving the edges unfinished or, if desired, blanket stitch around the edges by machine or by hand.

Make 12.

3. Sew the blocks into four rows of three blocks each, alternating pink checked blocks and light pink print blocks as shown. Press the seams in opposite directions and press the row seams in one direction.

4. Sew the 11" medium pink pieces to the top and bottom of the quilt, pressing the seams toward the borders. Sew the 17½" green pieces to the sides of the quilt and then press again.

FINISHING

1. Layer the quilt top, batting, and backing, and baste the layers together as shown in "Putting the Quilt Together" on page 76.

2. Quilt ⅟₁₆" away from the fused heart flowers and in the ditch around each block. Using a small lid or cup and a quilting pen or white pencil, trace a scalloped design from one block to the next in the green and pink borders. Quilt on the curved lines. Sew a button to the center of each heart flower.

3. Attach the binding to the quilt referring to "Single-Fold Binding" on page 77.

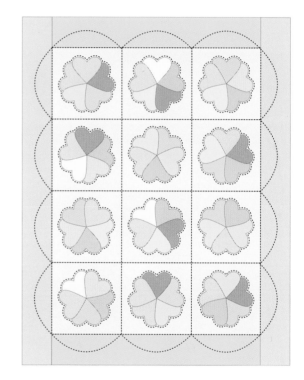

Heart
Cut 60.

Forties Pinwheels

Finished Quilt Size: 16½" x 20½" • Finished Block Size: 4" x 4"

With the arrival of World War II, quilting suffered another downturn as women entered the work force and fabric became scarce. Full of vintage charm, this simple little pinwheel quilt shows off its patriotic colors through 1940s reproduction prints.

MATERIALS

Yardages are based on 42"-wide, 100%-cotton fabrics.

¼ yard of white polka-dot fabric for blocks

¼ yard of medium blue 1940s reproduction fabric for borders

¼ yard *total* of 6 different blue 1940s reproduction fabrics for blocks

¼ yard *total* of 6 different red 1940s reproduction fabrics for blocks and corners

⅝ yard of backing fabric

¼ yard of light blue print for binding

20" x 24" piece of batting

CUTTING

From *each* of the blue reproduction fabrics for blocks, cut:
2 squares, 2⅞" x 2⅞" (12 squares total)

From *each* of the red reproduction fabrics, cut:
2 squares, 2⅞" x 2⅞" (12 squares total)

From *1* of the red reproduction fabrics, cut:
4 squares, 2½" x 2½"

From the white polka-dot fabric, cut:
24 squares, 2⅞" x 2⅞"

From the medium blue reproduction fabric for borders, cut:
2 strips, 2½" x 42"; crosscut into 2 pieces, 2½" x 12½", and 2 pieces, 2½" x 16½"

From the light blue print, cut:
2 strips, 1⅜" x 42"

ASSEMBLY

1. Pair each 2⅞" square of red and blue with a white polka-dot 2⅞" square, right sides together, with the white square on top. Draw a diagonal line across each white square. Stitch ¼" from the line on both sides, and cut on the drawn line. Press the seams toward the red or blue fabric.

Make 24 red and 24 blue.

2. Sew four matching triangle squares together as shown to make each Pinwheel block, pressing the seam for each pair in opposite directions toward the blue or red triangle as shown and pressing the final seam in either direction.

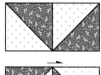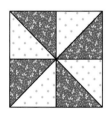

Make 6 red and 6 blue.

3. Arrange the blocks in four rows of three blocks each as shown, alternating red and blue pinwheels. Sew the blocks into rows and press the seams in the opposite direction from row to row. Sew the rows together and press the seams in one direction.

4. Sew the two 16½" medium blue pieces to the sides of the quilt center and press the seams toward the borders.

5. Sew the four 2½" red squares to each end of the two 12½" medium blue pieces. Press the seams toward the blue. Sew these border strips to the top and bottom of the quilt center and press the seams toward the borders.

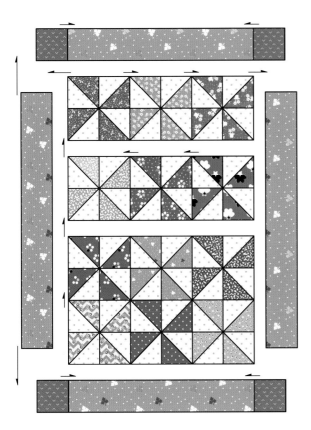

FINISHING

1. Layer the quilt top, batting, and backing, and baste the layers together as shown in "Putting the Quilt Together" on page 76.

2. Quilt an on-point square at the center of each pinwheel block. Quilt an X in each of the red corners. You may choose to quilt in the ditch along the inside edge of the blue borders as well.

3. Attach the binding to the quilt referring to "Single-Fold Binding" on page 77.

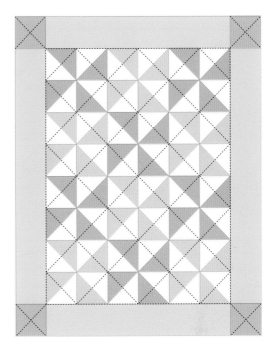

Quilting Basics

All of the quilts in this book can be made using a basic sewing machine and finishing by hand. If you are a beginner, start by choosing one of the easier projects and work your way up to the more challenging quilts; you will see your progress as you finish each quilt, and you'll be learning basic blocks and skills in the same way beginners did years ago. Have fun making your quilts!

QUILTMAKING TIPS

- Start small. Choose some of the simpler designs in this book, such as "Prairie Quilt" on page 26 or "Civil War Nine Patch" on page 46, to begin with (especially if you're teaching a child); then progress to the other patterns.

- Don't be afraid to make mistakes—every quilter has to begin somewhere. Have fun! The more quilts you make, the more experienced you'll become.

- Your stitches don't have to be perfect to make a perfectly darling quilt.

- Be creative! Combine fabric colors you wouldn't normally think of sewing next to each other. Make no two blocks the same, and use up all your scraps. If you're looking for a calming effect, use lots of blue.

- Remember that the joy of quilting is in the creating and the satisfaction is in the learning. Let children (as well as older beginners) progress at their own pace and make mistakes they can learn from. Give positive reinforcement. Saying "See what you can do?" encourages the love of quilting.

TOOLS

Here are a few tools you'll need to begin your quilt projects.

- **Rotary cutter:** A medium-sized cutter (45 mm) will enable you to cut strips and trim small pieces.

- **Ruler:** You will need a clear plastic ruler for cutting fabric. Choose one that is at least 4" x 12" with measurements clearly marked. A 6" square ruler comes in handy too.

- **Cutting mat:** You will use this gridded surface for cutting fabric. The 18" x 24" size is a good choice.

- **Pins:** You will need sharp pins to hold your pieces for sewing.

- **Needles:** Use 80/12 sewing machine needles for machine piecing. Change your needle after every major project to be sure your needle is always sharp. You will need basic hand-sewing needles for turning bindings and needles called Betweens for hand quilting.

- **Thread:** Always use 100%-cotton thread for your piecing, and use quilting thread, which is coated for extra strength, for hand quilting. A neutral color like tan blends well with most fabrics.

- **Seam ripper:** Expect to make some mistakes, and don't worry too much about them. When there's a mistake you just can't live with, a seam ripper can be your best friend.

- **Iron and pressing surface:** Any iron with a cotton setting will work for pressing your quilt pieces. You will need a flat surface for pressing, such as an ironing board or pressing mat.

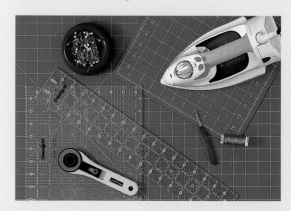

ROTARY CUTTING

Accurate cutting is an important part of making a quilt. If your pieces are not cut properly, the piecing will be difficult and all the measurements will be off. Cutting is also important for conserving your fabric. While strip cutting doesn't work too well with scrap quilts because no two blocks are usually the same, you *can* layer your different fabrics and cut multiple fabrics at the same time. Any strips that are required for these small quilts are cut across the grain of the fabric.

SEAM ALLOWANCES

Use a ¼" seam allowance and strive for accuracy. Even a slight ⅛" variance in block size will make a difference in your small quilts and you may find it difficult to fit the pieces together the right way. If your machine does not have a ¼" foot, place a strip of masking tape on the throat plate exactly ¼" away from the needle and use this as a guide while you sew.

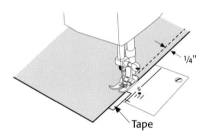

1/4"

Tape

REGARDING ACCURACY

Remember that while accuracy is important, these small quilts need not be perfect to be pleasing. Doll quilts made by children long ago weren't perfect, and their charm is that much more evident.

SIMPLE BLOCKS

To simplify sewing, squares and triangles are sewn into larger units called blocks. Blocks are usually square and are then pieced together to form the top of the quilt. Most of the quilts in this book use the following simple blocks: four patch, nine patch, triangle square, hourglass, and flying geese.

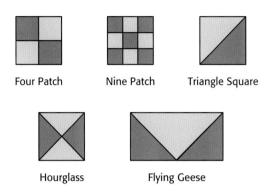

Four Patch   Nine Patch   Triangle Square

Hourglass   Flying Geese

PRESSING

Most quilters press sewn seams to one side, toward the darker fabric if possible. To join pieces, blocks, or rows of blocks, press the seams in opposite directions to make opposing seams. Pressing in this way allows seams to line up more easily and the blocks will fit together nicely.

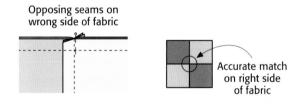

Opposing seams on wrong side of fabric

Accurate match on right side of fabric

FUSIBLE APPLIQUÉ

Using a lightweight, double-sided fusible-web product, trace your shape onto the paper side. Cut out the shape ¼" away from the lines. Peel off the paper backing and fuse to the wrong side of your fabric, following the product directions. Cut out the fabric shape and position it in place on the background fabric. Fuse, again following the product directions since each product is different. Leave as is or, if desired, machine finish with a zigzag stitch or hand finish with a buttonhole stitch. To give more depth to fused appliqué pieces, I like to hand quilt around each shape, ¹⁄₁₆" from the edge, after the quilt top, backing, and batting have been layered.

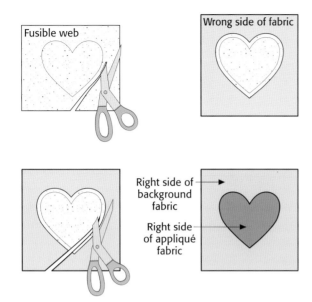

ADDING BORDERS

Think of the quilt as a picture. The border frames it and provides an important complement to the quilt picture. The colors in the border should offset the colors in the main body of the quilt and not detract the eye or overshadow the whole picture. It is always important to measure the sewn quilt top before cutting the border strips. Measure the length of the quilt top through the center. Cut your side borders to this measurement. Then measure the width of the quilt top through the center, including the side borders you just added. Cut your top and bottom borders to this measurement. This way, you will avoid cutting a strip too short and not having enough fabric left to cut another.

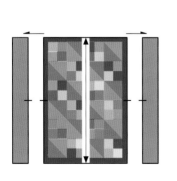
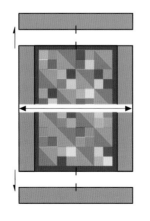

PUTTING THE QUILT TOGETHER

If needed, square up the four corners of your quilt top using a square ruler. Trim the four sides, if necessary, by lining up your long ruler from one corner to the opposite corner and trimming off any excess fabric.

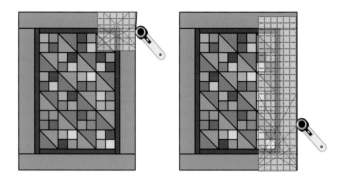

Use a low-loft cotton batting for the soft, flat look found in many antique quilts. Cut the batting and backing at least 3" larger in length and width than the quilt top. Lay the backing on a smooth, clean surface. Keeping it taut but not stretched, secure the backing to the surface with masking tape. Layer the batting and quilt top over the backing. Baste or pin the layers together.

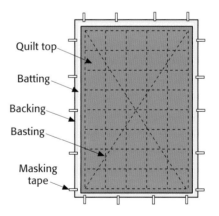

QUILTING

These small quilts require only the simplest of quilting, and I have chosen to quilt them by hand. You may prefer to quilt them by machine using similar quilting patterns. I have used simple quilting designs because more elaborate quilting patterns may dominate the quilts and detract from their simplicity. Quilting by hand is one of the simplest of needlework skills, requiring merely a little practice, and the result provides a delightful homespun touch. I love to quilt by hand because it gives me an opportunity to slow down and savor all of the wonderful colors and designs in the fabrics chosen for the quilt. Use an 18" length of a neutral-colored quilting thread (or black if you're making "Amish Nine Patch" on page 63) and make the smallest, most even stitches you can.

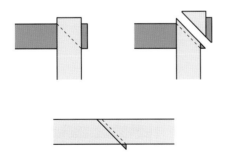

SINGLE-FOLD BINDING

1. From the binding fabric, cut 1⅜"-wide strips across the grain. The number of strips you need is calculated by measuring around all four edges of your quilt and adding a couple of extra inches (which can be cut off later) for good measure. Divide this number by 40 (the number of useable inches from one strip of fabric), and round up to the nearest whole number. The number of binding strips you'll need to cut for each of the quilts in this book, however, has been indicated for you in the project instructions. Sew the strips together at a 45° angle as shown and press the seams to one side.

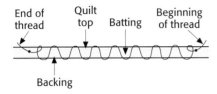

2. Using your ruler, make sure the corners form right angles, and straighten the edges of the quilt as necessary (refer to "Putting the Quilt Together" on page 76). Trim away excess batting and backing. Fold over ¼" at one end of the binding strip and press, wrong sides together. Starting with the folded end, position the binding on the quilt, right sides together, and align the raw edges. Stitch the binding to the quilt top, starting at the center of one side and

using a ¼" seam. Sew through all three layers. Stop ¼" away from the first corner and backstitch.

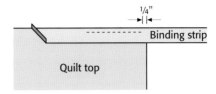

3. Remove the quilt from the machine. Turn the quilt and fold the binding straight up, making a 45° angle. Fold the binding back down, aligning it with the edge of the next side. Continue sewing the remaining sides in this way. When you come to the place where you started, stitch over the end you folded at the beginning, and clip the excess.

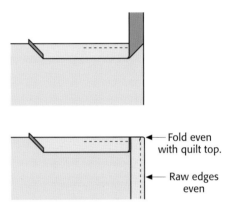

4. Fold the binding over to the back of the quilt. Turn the raw edge under ¼" and slip-stitch it to the back of the quilt using matching thread. Miter each of the corners as shown.

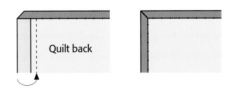

ADDING THE QUILT LABEL

Provide a nice finishing touch by adding your name and date to the back of the quilt, writing on a small piece of muslin with a permanent fine-tipped marker, and sewing the muslin to the quilt back.

Bibliography

Atkins, Jacqueline Marx. *Shared Threads, Quilting Together—Past and Present.* New York: Viking Studio Books, 1994.

Bishop, Robert, and Carleton L. Safford. *America's Quilts and Coverlets.* New York: Weathervane Books, 1974.

Brackman, Barbara. *Quilts from the Civil War.* Lafayette, CA: C & T Publishing, 1997.

Cobb, Mary. *Quilt Block History of Pioneer Days.* Brookfield, CT: Millbrook Press, 1995.

Duke, Dennis, and Deborah Harding, eds. *America's Glorious Quilts.* New York: Hugh Lauter Levin Associates, Inc., 1987.

Ferrero, Pat, Elaine Hedges, and Julie Silber. *Hearts and Hands: The Influence of Women and Quilts on American Society.* San Francisco, CA: Quilt Digest Press, 1987.

Fox, Sandi. *Small Endearments: 19th Century Quilts for Children and Dolls.* New York: Charles Scribner's Sons, 1985.

Gallagher, Susan Bennett. *Childhood Dreams.* New York: Sterling Publishing Co., 1989.

Greenstein, Blanche, and Thomas K. Woodard. *Crib Quilts and Other Small Wonders.* New York: E.P. Dutton, 1981.

Johnson, Anne. *America's Quilting History.* www.womenfolk.com/historyofquilts, 2001.

Kiracofe, Roderick. *The American Quilt: A History of Cloth and Comfort 1750–1950.* New York: Clarkson Potter, 1993.

Kolter, Jane Bentley. *Forget Me Not: A Gallery of Friendship and Album Quilts.* Pittstown, NJ: Main Street Press, 1985.

Lasansky, Jeanette. *Pieced by Mother: Over 100 Years of Quiltmaking Traditions.* Lewisburg, PA: Union County Historical Society, 1987.

Levie, Eleanor. *Great Little Quilts.* New York: Harry N. Abrams, Inc., 1990.

Orlofsky, Patsy and Myron Orlofsky. *Quilts in America.* New York: McGraw-Hill, 1974.

Shaw, Robert. *Quilts, A Living Tradition.* New York: Hugh Lauter Levin Associates, Inc., 1995.

Trestain, Eileen. *Dating Fabrics: A Color Guide, 1800–1960.* Paducah, KY: American Quilter's Society, 1998.

Waldvogel, Merikay. *Soft Covers for Hard Times.* Nashville, TN: Rutledge Hill Press, 1990.

Wilens, Patricia, ed. *America's Heritage Quilts.* Des Moines, IA: Meredith Corporation, 1991.

Wulfert, Kimberly. *New Pathways into Quilt History.* www.antiquequiltdating.com, 2002.

About the Author

Kathleen Tracy began her quilting career by making quilts for her daughter's dolls and bears. Small quilts with an antique look fascinated her, and she began designing her own patterns in the colors she loved. She started her own pattern and quilt-kit business, Country Lane Quilts, to give new quilters the convenience of simple design and old-fashioned fabrics combined. Kathleen lives in Deerfield, Illinois, with her husband, Paul, her son and daughter, Evan and Caitlin, and her Wheaten Terrier, Rigby.

See more quilts and patterns at www.countrylanequilts.com.

New and Bestselling Titles from

Martingale®
& COMPANY
America's Best-Loved Craft & Hobby Books®
America's Best-Loved Knitting Books®

America's Best-Loved Quilt Books®

NEW RELEASES
300 Paper-Pieced Quilt Blocks
American Doll Quilts
Classic Crocheted Vests
Dazzling Knits
Follow-the-Line Quilting Designs
Growing Up with Quilts
Hooked on Triangles
Knitting with Hand-Dyed Yarns
Lavish Lace
Layer by Layer
Lickety-Split Quilts
Magic of Quiltmaking, The
More Nickel Quilts
More Reversible Quilts
No-Sweat Flannel Quilts
One-of-a-Kind Quilt Labels
Patchwork Showcase
Pieced to Fit
Pillow Party!
Pursenalities
Quilter's Bounty
Quilting with My Sister
Seasonal Quilts Using Quick Bias
Two-Block Appliqué Quilts
Ultimate Knitted Tee, The
Vintage Workshop, The
WOW! Wool-on-Wool Folk Art Quilts

APPLIQUÉ
Appliquilt in the Cabin
Blossoms in Winter
Garden Party
Shadow Appliqué
Stitch and Split Appliqué
Sunbonnet Sue All through the Year

Our books are available at
bookstores and your favorite
craft, fabric, and yarn retailers.
If you don't see the title
you're looking for, visit us at
www.martingale-pub.com
or contact us at:

1-800-426-3126

International: 1-425-483-3313
Fax: 1-425-486-7596
Email: info@martingale-pub.com

6/04

HOLIDAY QUILTS & CRAFTS
Christmas Cats and Dogs
Christmas Delights
Hocus Pocus!
Make Room for Christmas Quilts
Welcome to the North Pole

LEARNING TO QUILT
101 Fabulous Rotary-Cut Quilts
Happy Endings, Revised Edition
Loving Stitches, Revised Edition
More Fat Quarter Quilts
Quilter's Quick Reference Guide, The
Sensational Settings, Revised Edition
Simple Joys of Quilting, The
Your First Quilt Book (or it should be!)

PAPER PIECING
40 Bright and Bold Paper-Pieced Blocks
50 Fabulous Paper-Pieced Stars
Down in the Valley
Easy Machine Paper Piecing
For the Birds
Papers for Foundation Piecing
Quilter's Ark, A
Show Me How to Paper Piece
Traditional Quilts to Paper Piece

QUILTS FOR BABIES & CHILDREN
Easy Paper-Pieced Baby Quilts
Easy Paper-Pieced Miniatures
Even More Quilts for Baby
More Quilts for Baby
Quilts for Baby
Sweet and Simple Baby Quilts

ROTARY CUTTING/SPEED PIECING
365 Quilt Blocks a Year Perpetual
   Calendar
1000 Great Quilt Blocks
Burgoyne Surrounded
Clever Quarters
Clever Quilts Encore
Endless Stars
Once More around the Block
Pairing Up
Stack a New Deck
Star-Studded Quilts
Strips and Strings
Triangle-Free Quilts

SCRAP QUILTS
Easy Stash Quilts
Nickel Quilts
Rich Traditions
Scrap Frenzy
Successful Scrap Quilts

TOPICS IN QUILTMAKING
Asian Elegance
Batiks and Beyond
Bed and Breakfast Quilts
Coffee-Time Quilts
Dutch Treat
English Cottage Quilts
Fast-Forward Your Quilting
Machine-Embroidered Quilts
Mad about Plaid!
Romantic Quilts
Simple Blessings

CRAFTS
20 Decorated Baskets
Beaded Elegance
Blissful Bath, The
Collage Cards
Creating with Paint
Holidays at Home
Pretty and Posh
Purely Primitive
Stamp in Color
Trashformations
Warm Up to Wool
Year of Cats…in Hats!, A

KNITTING & CROCHET
365 Knitting Stitches a Year Perpetual
   Calendar
Beyond Wool
Classic Knitted Vests
Crocheted Aran Sweaters
Crocheted Lace
Crocheted Socks!
Garden Stroll, A
Knit it Now!
Knits for Children and Their Teddies
Knits from the Heart
Knitted Throws and More
Knitter's Template, A
Little Box of Scarves, The
Little Box of Sweaters, The
Style at Large
Today's Crochet
Too Cute! Cotton Knits for Toddlers